Thus We Keep Faith

Thus We Keep Faith

The Operational History of 196 Squadron RAF

1942-1946

Steve Holmes

www.bombercommandbooks.com

This edition first published 2021 by Mention the War Ltd., 25 Cromwell Street, Merthyr Tydfil, CF47 8RY.

Copyright 2021 © Steve Holmes.

The right of Steve Holmes to be identified as Author of this work is asserted by him in accordance with the Copyright, Designs and Patents Act 1988.

The original Operational Record Books of 196 Squadron are Crown Copyright and stored in microfiche and digital format by the National Archives. Material is reproduced under Open Licence v.3.0.

All rights reserved. No part of this publication may be reproduced, stored in a retrieval system, transmitted in any form or by any means, electronic, mechanical or photocopied, recorded or otherwise, without the written permission of the copyright owners.

This squadron profile has been researched, compiled and written by its author, who has made every effort to ensure the accuracy of the information contained in it. The author will not be liable for any damages caused, or alleged to be caused, by any information contained in this book. E. & O.E.

Cover design: Topics - The Creative Partnership www.topicsdesign.co.uk

A CIP catalogue reference for this book is available from the British Library.

ISBN 9781911255697

Also by Steve Holmes:

Sherlock's Squadron

Contents

Dedication 9
Introduction 10
Acknowledgements 11
Glossary of Terms and Abbreviations 12
Early History 16
Reformation and World War II 16
January 1943 18
February 1943 20
March 1943 27
April 1943 34
May 1943 42
June 1943 47
July 1943 57
August 1943 62
September 1943 66
October 1943 70
November 1943 74
December 1943 76
January 1944 78
February 1944 80
March 1944 85
April 1944 88
May 1944 91
June 1944 94
July 1944 103
August 1944 106
September 1944 113
October 1944 143

November 1944	145
December 1944	147
January 1945	150
February 1945	152
March 1945	161
April 1945	172
May 1945	176
June 1945	182
July 1945	185
August 1945	187
September 1945	194
October 1945	196
November 1945	199
December 1945	201
January 1946	203
February 1946	207
March 1946	208
Appendix I: Aircraft	213
Vickers Wellington Mk X	213
Short Stirling Mks III, IV and V	215
Appendix II: Sorties	219
Appendix III: 196 Squadron Roll of Honour 1942-1946	221
Bibliography	231

Dedication

To all the 196 Squadron crew members of different nationalities who served from all over the world and who gave their lives in order for us all to be free.

Introduction

It was my father's stories as a boy which in later life drew me to the fascination of the Short Stirling. It wasn't until a few years after his death in 1985 that I decided to try and research his history in 196 Squadron. Starting with only his service number I set out to find what I could. Bearing in mind that this was before most people had the help of the internet and Google, a lot of my research was done by normal snail mail post. Looking back now, it's incredible how much time things took.

After a while, when everyone had started to get access to the internet, things did speed up. It took me fifteen years before I thought that I had probably enough material to write about my father and his crew which culminated in the publication of my book, *Sherlock's Squadron*.

After this, I thought about the other airmen and crews, wondering what happened to them. I decided to find out and write a history of the squadron.

I didn't realise the work entailed, the time it would consume, and the dedication needed to keep going when the times got tough. To say it was mentally challenging is an understatement. It can take a lot of time searching for one little bit of information or possibly a photograph on a certain subject. Then there is the temptation to go off on a tangent when unearthing other interesting facts. It has taken me two years to collate all the information, stories and photos, as well as the statistics of the squadron, to be found at the end of the book.

This book is told from the daily running of the squadron, based on the Operation Record Books and the daily summaries that were recorded at the time. These were very brief but led to the real work, tracking down stories that concurred with the records.

Much of this information and photographs came from the internet, but over the years I have tracked down and contacted so many relations of the airmen in 196 Squadron. Many people have been kind enough to share their stories with me and provide some great stories and photos of their relatives. In turn, I, hope I have given some people information they didn't already have. Other invaluable information has come from books on the subject, to whose authors I am indebted.

Seventy-six years have passed since the end of World War Two, but the interest in the aviation side is immense and I hope this book is an addition to its history.

Steve Holmes,

Finestrat, Spain, January 2021

Acknowledgements

I am indeed indebted to the following people whose help given in the writing of this book has been invaluable. Without them this book could not have been written.

Graham Howard, Gregory Lunt, Benoit Howson, Leo Janssen, Peter Hurrell, Robert Franklin, Malcolm Schaverien, Danielle Park, Andrew White, Simon Sommerville, Russ+Bev Tickner, The Camerons, Robert Caldwell, Judy Vanrenen, Mike Stimpson, Sally+Richard Hanlon, Neil Westoby, Diana Phillips, Sue Thompson, Lesley Smith, Ian Austin, Aircrew Remembered, Alan and Jackie Hunt, John Reid, Warren Tickner, Bruce Gommersall, Bruno Lecaplain, Jonny Graf, Mike Stimpson, Charlie King, The Tammas Family, Duncan Oldham, Ken Scott, Steve Smith, Chris Chandler.

Glossary of Terms and Abbreviations

A/C	Aircraft
AEAF.	Allied Expeditionary Air Force
A/B	Bomb Aimer or Bombadier
A.S.R.S.	Air Sea Rescue Service
A.T.C.	Air Training Corps
C-in-C	Commander-in –Chief
C.O.	Commanding Officer
C.U.	Conversion Unit
DFC	Distinguished Flying Cross
DFM	Distinguished Flying Medal
DSO	Distinguished Service Order
DZ	Drop Zone (for paratrooper and air-dropped supplies)
F/E	Flight Engineer
F/O	Flying Officer
F/Ltn	Flight Lieutenant
F/Sgt	Flight Sergeant
F.T.R.	Failed to Return
GEE	Radio Navigation Aid
HCU	Heavy Conversion Unit
LZ	Landing Zone
Mk	Mark as in Stirling Mk III
NCO	Non-Commissioned Officer
NZ	New Zealand
ORB	Operation Record Book
O.T.U.	Operation Training Unit

p/i	Port Inner
p/o	Port Outer
P/O	Pilot Officer
RCAF	Royal Canadian Air Force
SAS	Special Air Service
Sgt	Sergeant
s/i	Starboard Inner
s/o	Starboard Outer
SOC	Struck Off Charge
SOE	Special Operations Executive
S/Ldr	Squadron Leader
S.S.Q.	Squadron Sick Quarters
u/s	Unserviceable
W/Cdr	Wing Commander
W/O	Warrant Officer
W/OP	Wireless Operator
W/T	Wireless Telegraphy

SIC FIDEM SERVAMUS - THUS WE KEEP FAITH

The Badge refers to some of the squadron's wartime functions, the mailed fist indicating the power of its bombing and the dagger being handed hilt down from the sky indicating its supply dropping activities

Early History

The first 196 Squadron was originally formed as a training unit at Heliopolis, Egypt on the 9th August 1917 and disbanded a mere 3 months later on 13th November 1917 becoming part of the Aerial Fighting School.

Reformation and World War II

From the outset of World War II, both Britain and Germany refrained from bombing civilian targets or cities. That was until, in August of 1940, Luftwaffe night bombers unintentionally (and against orders) attacked London. Winston Churchill immediately ordered retaliatory raids on Berlin, this enraged Hitler to order intensified bombing of targets in and around London and other British cities. Both sides thus claimed that their attacks on enemy cities were in retaliation for what had been begun by the enemy.

In the event of escalating raids, Bomber Command was in need of more Bomber Squadrons. Thus on the 7th of November 1942, 196 Squadron was formed at Driffield, East Yorkshire as a Night Bomber Squadron, as part of No. 4 Group Bomber Command. Driffield was located 1.7 miles south west of Driffield village and 10.7 miles North West of Beverley. The squadron was to be equipped with Vickers Wellington Mk III aircraft. The Commanding Officer at Driffield was Wing Commander R.H. Waterhouse A.F.C.

Richard Henry Waterhouse was born in the Sunderland area on the 5th May 1913. He was commissioned in 1933. He appears to have been attached to the RCAF for exchange duties in 1939. On 20 August 1939 he was temporarily appointed a Flight Lieutenant in the RCAF. He was posted to Camp Borden on 31 August 1939, and promptly relinquished his RCAF commission; such records as had been generated in that period were placed on his RAF file. He attained the rank of Squadron Leader in 1940, and Acting Group Captain in 1943. In September 1942 he ferried an aircraft (FL945) to England via Montreal and Goose Bay; the Ferry Command crew card gives his home as Moorfields, Cotherstone, Yorkshire, although his wife at that time gave her address as 37 Holland Street, Kitchener, Ontario, which was consistent with him being stationed at Brantford.

In the first few weeks the squadron proceeded to welcome new aircrew. Their time was spent with schedule of training as laid down by No. 4 Group, also watching various training films, as up to now no aircraft had arrived at the station. Aircrews, apart from training, had sports organised for them and some even helped with the local farmers in growing their produce. The squadron now had around 19 crews formed. On the 1st December, the squadron took delivery of the first four aircraft, two Wellington Mk IIIs and two Mk Xs. Subsequently the Mk IIIs were exchanged for two MK Xs from 429 Squadron, which resulted in the first flights of the squadron on the 3rd December. By mid- December the crews numbered 26.

The Vickers Wellington's chief designer at Vickers Weybridge works was Rex Pierson, but the unique feature of the Wellington, its geodetic construction, was the brainchild of Dr. Barnes Wallis who went on to develop the bouncing bomb for the Dambuster raids. The Wellington was a twin engine, long range medium bomber and at the time of the formation of the squadron, was the mainstay of the Royal Air Force. It was powered by two Bristol Hercules radial engines and had a top speed of around 255 mph and had a service ceiling of 22,000 feet and a range of 1200 miles with a maximum payload. As well as being able to carry up to 4000lb of bombs it was also equipped to carry torpedoes and could also be used for mine laying. It was affectionately known as the Wimpy by service personnel after J. Wellington Wimpy from the Popeye cartoons.

On the 22nd December the Squadron moved to R.A.F. Leconfield, East Yorkshire. An early expansion scheme aerodrome in the East Riding, Leconfield was laid out on an area of level meadowland, between the LNER line from Beverley to Great Driffield in the east and the A614 road to the same locations in the west. Construction began in 1935 to the common design of the period, the permanent barrack, administrative and technical buildings being located in close proximity on the west side of the flying field adjacent to Leconfield village. Four Type C hangars fronted the bombing circle with a fifth to the rear at the southern end. Also at the same time, 22nd December, 466 Squadron an Australian based unit also moved to Leconfield. This was common practice to have two squadrons at one base being big enough to accommodate this.

On Christmas Eve aircrew were given a half day off. On Christmas day all except essential work on the squadron was suspended for the day. As far as possible Christmas Festivities were carried out. The senior N.C.O's visiting the Officers Mess at 11.00 hours and the compliment returned by the Officer's visiting the senior N.C.O's Mess, after which both officer's and senior N.C.O's had carried out the custom of waiting upon the airmen, in the Airmen's Mess for Christmas Dinner. For the rest of December, the squadron continued flying training, apart from the days with adverse weather conditions.

January 1943

For the biggest part of January the squadron's aircrew were training in accordance with the No.4 Group Syllabus.

It wasn't unusual, while waiting for the squadron's aircraft to be delivered, for 196 Squadron pilots to go on sorties with 466 Squadron, who were already operational, as second dickies, (second pilots). It was on two of these occasions that two pilots were lost.

14th January: HE152 from 466 Sqn took off on a minelaying op. to 'Nectarine's. Flying as second dickie was Sgt. John Albert Austin RNZAF of 196 Sqn. The aircraft was hit by flak and crashed into the sea west of Armeland. This was 466 Squadron's first operational loss. All of the crew are remembered on the Runnymede Memorial.

21st January: HE410 of 466Sqn was on a minelaying operation to Terschelling. Second dickie this day was Sgt. William Robert Fisher. It was hit by flak which caused it to lose height and hit a telegraph pole near Mantgum, then crashing near Leeuwarden. Ironically out of all the crew Sgt Fisher was the only one to be killed, all the rest being taken as POWs.

29th January: On their first official sortie, five aircraft were dispatched on a sea search for the missing crew of another squadron, but no aircraft were successful in the search.

30th January: Six aircraft were sent out for a second day but no results were obtained.

In January the squadron flew a total of 11 sorties with the loss of no aircraft but two aircrew.

Sgt. J.A. Austin RNZAF

Sgt. R.W. Fisher RAF

Remains of Wellington HE410

February 1943

The codes allocated to the squadron were **ZO** (Nov 42 – Mar 46) **5T** and **7T** (May 43 – Mar 46.)

The first sorties flown in earnest by the squadron were on the 4/5th February 1943. The target was Lorient in Brittany, France. Lorient was the location of a German U-boat base. Admiral Karl Donitz decided to construct the base on 28 June 1940. Between February 1941 and January 1942 three gigantic reinforced concrete structures were built on the Keroman peninsula. They were called K1, K2 and K3. The base was capable of sheltering thirty submarines under cover. Since they could not destroy the base and its submarine pens, the Allies had decided to flatten the city and port of Lorient, in order to cut the supply lines to the U-boat bases.

4th February: Nine aircraft from 196 Squadron were detailed for the raid on Lorient. First up at 18.24hrs was W/C Waterhouse in Wellington HE168, followed at two-minute intervals by the other eight aircraft. The payload of all eight aircraft was 2x1000lb and 3x500lb bombs. The first few aircraft arrived and dropped their bomb at around 21.20hrs from between 10,000 and 12,000ft in excellent visibility, but the last 3 aircraft encountered poor visibility due to smoke rising from the fires below, but despite this all aircraft dropped their loads over target. All aircraft reported an excellent trip with no encounters with enemy aircraft arriving back at base between 00.15-01.10hrs.

There was one exception though, aircraft HE398 piloted by W/O Ritchie encountered severe swing to starboard on take-off. The aircraft went through a dummy hedge and lost one blade off the starboard propeller. Take off was made and the aircraft circled the aerodrome until all clear, when a good landing with all bombs was made. There was considerable damage to aircraft caused by starboard engine vibration A total of 120 aircraft out of the 128 dropped their bombs over the target

U-36 sails into its pen in Lorient. When birthed inside these bunkers, the U-boats were safe from air raids.

that night, with only one loss, a Lancaster Bomber of 427 Squadron. In all a total of 90 tons of bombs were dropped on Lorient in the raid.

7th February: Operations again to Lorient by 11 aircraft from the squadron. First aircraft took off at 19.01hrs. Payload of each aircraft in tonight's raid was 7x500lb. All aircraft was successful over the target reporting vast fires over the area. All aircraft returned to base safely with no enemy aircraft sighted.

12th February: The squadron was detailed on mine-laying operations. Six aircraft took off from the base at 18.55hrs onwards. Target for tonight is to lay mines off the Frisian Islands. Each aircraft carrying 2x1500lb sea mines. Visibility was excellent, due to bright moonlight, and all mines were dropped from 800ft and planted correctly. One exception being HE385 piloted by F/O Eastwood whose aircraft was unable to take off due to a defect in the bomb release mechanism. These mining missions were known as 'Gardening'.

13th February: Eleven aircraft detailed to bomb Lorient again. Bomb load tonight was 2x500lb bombs and 540x4lb incendiaries. Operation as previous, but much more light and heavy flak was encountered than on previous raids, but still no enemy aircraft encountered. All aircraft had good trips and returned to base safely.

14th February: The squadron was dispatched to bomb Cologne. Until then the squadron had suffered very little enemy action in the raids undertaken to date, but for the first time they were to fly over a heavily defended Germany. The squadron sent 11 aircraft as part of the Bomber Command strength of 243 aircraft that night. The squadrons payload for the trip varied from incendiaries, 500 pounders and 1x4000 pounder dropped from 15,000ft from Wellington HE166 piloted by F/O Eastwood.

Wellington HE 469 piloted by F/Lt Bonard was attacked by an enemy fighter and was badly damaged putting, large holes in both wings and damaging the port engine and undercarriage. The aircraft managed to then elude the fighter and head for home. Owing to the damage by the night fighter, the aircraft crash landed back at base, but fortunately the crew suffered no serious injuries

Wellington HE169 piloted by F/Lt. R.F. Milne was, as stated in the Operations Record Books (ORBs) 'Aircraft did not return from operation and no report can be given.'

The crew of HE169 was: Pilot: F/Lt Roderick Fairweather Milne RNZAF. Nav: P/O David Morgan Frost RCAF. A/B: F/O Thomas Clinton Stuart Wood RCAF. W/Op: W/O Greaves Glenn Clark RCAF. A/G: F/Sgt John Duncan McIntyre.

P/O Thomas Stuart Clinton Wood

All the men are remembered on the Runnymede Memorial. It later emerged that the aircraft was intercepted and attacked over the North Sea by a Messerschmitt Bf 110 around 21.50hrs and plunged into the sea 20 miles west of Schouwen, Holland, with all the crew perishing. The Me110 was piloted by Oberleutnant Paul Gildner. Gildner was one of the Luftwaffe's top aces.

16th February: Five aircraft took off on mine-laying duties in the 'Jellyfish' area. Each aircraft carrying 2x1500lb mines which were dropped from heights between 500 and 800ft. Visibility was good, and the target was pinpointed by the lighthouse and square tower at Pointe Du Toulinguet. All aircraft were successful, and all had a satisfactory trip, apart from Wellington HE385, which was piloted by F/O Culff. His aircraft was attacked by an enemy aircraft. The tail plane was damaged causing the intercom to become u/s to the rear gunner. All aircraft returned to base safely.

On the same night 2 aircraft were sent to again bomb Lorient. Each aircraft carrying 3x500lb bombs, 450x4lb and 8x30lb bombs. The target was identified by the River Scorff and the load dropped from 14000ft. Wellington HE166 piloted by F/O Eastwood had a successful trip apart from the escape hatch being open throughout the trip. The other aircraft HE412 piloted by Sgt Morgan, at about 2200hrs, had problems with their oxygen supply at around 7000ft. Having dropped to 4000ft by 23.00hrs, the crew were suffering from a dopey effect. The flow meters had been flickering the whole trip. The oxygen supply was set as for 20000ft but was still insufficient. Despite this the aircraft landed safely at base.

17th February: Three aircraft went to join a formation of other squadron aircrafts to bomb Emden, carrying 6x500lb bombs. Wellington HE165 piloted by P/O Hope visually identified the target by the Ems Estuary, but a momentary failure of intercom caused the captain to go back into the clouds. Repair was adjusted in 5 minutes but coming out of the cloud they could not locate Nordeen again, and seeing a small town on the edge of a railway, bombed it. Wellington HE179 piloted by F/O Wilson found conflicting fixes and winds, and was uncertain if he was over Holland, so returned to base making a safe landing with a full bomb load.

18th February: Crews were given a half day off. Aircrew played a soccer match against the ground crew

19th February: Nine aircraft joined a formation to bomb Wilshelmshaven. They carried various bombs and incendiaries. All aircraft had successful trips, apart from Wellington HE398 piloted by Sgt Duckmanton, who took off but landed immediately owing to the constant speed indicator being u/s. It was noted by F/O Culff that a great many aircraft seem to be early and to be circling over rendezvous point to waste time.

The squadron had a brief respite after a hectic 3 weeks of near constant operations.

The squadron was due on ops on the 21st, 22nd, and the 24th but were stood down due to adverse weather conditions.

25th February: Squadron detailed on a mine-laying mission. Ten aircraft taking off for the 'Nectarine' area. All aircraft again carrying 2x1500 mines and dropped from between 2000 and 5000ft. Eight of the aircraft successfully planted the mines, but Wellington HE378 piloted by Sgt Morgan, encountered bad visibility with 10/10ths cloud and decided that the drop zone was not reliable enough, the mines being returned safely to base. Wellington HE166 also encountered the same cloud and dropped to 200ft but decided not to plant the mines, he also safely returned to base with his load.

Wellington HF464 ZO-H. This photo was taken in late 1942 and is probably one of the first to be taken of 196 Squadron. The original photo was signed on the front, presumably by the crew. J.W Beale, W.F Templett and F.Elliott. On the back is the name 'Azzaro' which is more than likely referring to Sgt V.E Azzaro, Air Gunner who appears in another crew later.

26th February: Wellington HE161 was on an air test flight when it crashed 2 miles E of Middleton-on-the-Wolds, 7 miles south of Great Driffield, exploding on impact. The accident was attributed to the canvas bomb screen detaching and fouling the elevator control surfaces.

The aircraft took off from Leconfield airfield at around 10.45hrs to undertake a routine air test prior to an operational flight that evening when it was to have been used. During the flight, the crew tested the operation of the bomb bay doors, the doors were opened successfully, but while they were open a canvas curtain in the bomb bay detached and fell out of the fuselage, and was thrown by the slip-stream onto the I.F.F. aerial and slid along this until it became jammed in the tailplane elevators. It was thought that the crew realised that the canvas was fouling the aircraft's elevator and that the pilot had in fact managed to shake it clear. The canvas curtain was found some 2.5 miles from where the aircraft would eventually crash.

At 12.20hrs the Wellington dived into the ground and exploded around two miles east of Middleton on the Wolds, it was thought that although the canvas had been shaken out of the elevator in making a steep dive, there was not enough height left to pull out of the dive and it struck the ground. All on board were sadly killed.

Wellington HE161 was built to contract B.124362/40 by Vickers Armstrong's Ltd. at Hawarden and was awaiting collection in November 1942. In January 1943 it was taken on charge by 429 Squadron at East Moor but was almost immediately transferred to 196 Squadron at Leconfield. As a result of the crash on 26th February 1943, Cat.E2/FA damage was the damage assessment and it was written off.

The crew of HE161 was: Pilot: F/O Neville Smart, Nav: F/O Thomas Donald Gordon, A/B: F/O Robert Lowell Benson RCAF, W/Op: Sgt George Alexander Aitken Ranken, A/G: Sgt Dennis Herbert, Passenger - LAC Walter Robinson.

F/O Thomas Donald Mckinlay Gordon

F/O Robert Lowell Benson

26th February: Today saw a return to bombing duties. Eleven aircraft from the squadron was detailed to join a formation to bomb Cologne. The squadron tonight was carrying various bombs ranging from 500 pounders to 1x4000 pounder and various incendiaries. Of the 11 aircraft bombing that night, 7 were successful with the exceptions of Wellington's HE166, HE168, HE170 and HE412.

HE166 piloted by Sgt A. Lucas decided to return to base owing to the illness of his navigator, Sgt Barber, supplemented by the fact that the aircraft was late and off track.

HE168 pilot Sgt Fletcher decided to return owing to aircraft being late, due to late take off which would have made it impossible to reach the target in time. His bomb load of 3x500lb G.P. bombs, 360x4lb and 16x30lb incendiaries were jettisoned from 16.000ft into the sea.

HE170 piloted by F/O Wilson dropped his 1x500lb bomb and his load of incendiaries, but 2 of his 500lb bombs failed to release, and were taken back to base.

HE412 piloted by Sgt Temlett decided to return to base with his full pay-load, due to the Port C.S.U. being u/s owing to an oil leak.

28th February: Thirteen aircraft from the squadron were sent to bomb the town of St. Nazaire. All aircraft were carrying various bombs and incendiaries and dropped from around 14000ft. The mission was a success, but Wellington HE162, when returning home, was over the enemy coast when the rear escape hatch blew away. The transmitter on T.R.9 was u/s. The rear turret door stuck and the detonator plug on the indicator unit of Gee was u/s. This brought to an end the first month of the squadron's operations

The beginning of 1943 began with the meeting at Casablanca between President Roosevelt and Winston Churchill with their Combined Chiefs of Staff. The most important decision of the Casablanca Conference was the decision to embark upon a combined bombing offensive with the objective of 'the progressive destruction and dislocation of the German military, industrial and economic system, and the undermining of the German people to a point where their capacity for armed resistance is fatally weakened'. Sir Arthur Harris, the head of Bomber Command had no doubts as to his interpretation of this highly ambiguous statement

The month of February 1943 had seen 196 Squadron well and truly pitched in to the trauma of WWII and RAF Bomber Command.

The squadron had flown a total of 113 sorties with the loss of 2 aircraft HE169 and HE161 and 10 aircrew.

George Augustus Shotun Williams joined 196 Squadron on the 7th November 1942 after completing his training as a navigator in Stirlings. As a member of pilot J. A. Hope's crew, they were one of the first crews to fly on the 1st day of operations on 196. He flew a total of 29 sorties, 2 minelaying and 27 bombing sorties. On several occasions the crew were hit by flak but always made it home. He was briefly transferred to 1631 Sqn in July '43 and then transferred back to 196 in August '43. He was then again transferred out of the squadron in October 43. Later George was transferred to 75(NZ) Sqn in late 44, doing another 6 bombing sorties, his last one being on the 2nd Jan 45. George flew a remarkable 35 Sorties over 3 years.

George Williams seated 3rd from right, bottom.

March 1943

1st March: Five aircraft set off in the evening for gardening in the Rosemary area. All aircraft that night was carrying the customary 1x500lb mines all dropped from a range of 1000/5000ft. The target was attacked by visual on breakwater on N.W. end of Spiekeroog. All vegetables (mines) planted successfully.

HE170 piloted by Sgt Symes attacked the primary target from 1000ft but owing to the rear turret being u/s it was decided not to fly to the given pinpoint, so mines were planted in the vicinity of the garden.

2nd March: Six officers and six sergeants were detailed to act as bearers at the funerals of P/O Benson and Sgt Rankin killed in the crash on the 26th February. The internment took place at Beverley Cemetery at 14.00hrs. The other four personnel killed in the crash were all sent to their homes for private burial at the next of kin's request.

3th March: Eleven aircraft from the squadron rendezvous with other squadron aircraft making, a total of over 450 aircraft to attack Hamburg that night. The aircraft were carrying 500 pounders and various incendiaries and were dropped from 16000ft. Vast fires were reported over the target and S/Ldr Macpherson in Wellington HE183 made a special reconnaissance over the area and reported attack to be very successful. On the way back the glare from the fires could be seen when aircraft was passing over Heligoland.

HE387 piloted by Sgt Hitchins, on the outward journey, had to turn for home owing to the illness of his rear gunner F/Sgt Harper. The bomb load being jettisoned into the sea.

5th March: This saw the start of what 'Bomber' Harris had defined as the beginning of 'The Battle of the Ruhr'. Ten aircraft from the squadron made up a force of 442 aircraft for the raid on Essen. Three waves of bombers, a mixture of Wellingtons, Halifaxes, Stirlings and Lancaster's, dropped their incendiaries and time-delayed bombs in under an hour. Only 153 aircraft bombed within 3 miles of the aiming point despite the target area marking by the Pathfinders using Oboe.

Of the 10 aircraft from the squadron HE168 piloted by W/O Mellor turned back just before the Dutch Coast owing to the aircraft being unable to climb above 12000ft. All bombs being taken back to base safely.

HE398 piloted by P/O Hope, when some 30 miles from the enemy coast, witnessed an enormous explosion below. The aircraft felt a bump at 10000ft but saw no other aircraft. The aircraft was damaged on the underside and the bomb door was pulled off, but the captain continued the trip and bombed the target. It was later discovered that HE398 had collided with Wellington HZ256 of 466 Squadron.

For his actions on the night of 5th/6th March 1943, P/O Hope was awarded an immediate DFC, Gazetted on 30th March 1943. The citation reads:

'Flying Officer Hope was captain and pilot of an aircraft which was detailed to attack Essen one night in March 1943. While the target was still a distance of 200 miles away the aircraft was involved in a collision and severely damaged, making any evasive action which might become necessary well-nigh impossible. It was also found impracticable to climb much beyond 14,000 feet. Despite the serious handicaps, Flying Officer Hope, with grim determination, proceeded on his mission which he successfully accomplished. This incident is typical of the fine fighting spirit, courage, and devotion to duty which have characterised all this officer's operational flying.'

Apart from these two aircraft, the rest of the squadron had successful trips. LN432 piloted by F/O Wilson reported that fires were still visible fifty miles beyond the Dutch coast on return. One of the later aircraft coming back, HE179 piloted by Sgt Sneddon, reported to be able to see the glow from the fires 125 miles away on their return. The squadron once again fared very well as 14 aircraft were lost from other squadrons on the raid.

6th March: Ten aircraft were detailed for operations but were cancelled fifteen minutes before take-off due to adverse weather reports, likely to prevail at base when aircraft were due to return.

8th March: Air Tests were carried out.

9th March: Four aircraft went mine-laying in the 'Nectarine' area. Three were successful, but Wellington HE179 piloted by Sgt Sneddon could not find land to pinpoint the target area owing to base cloud, and mines were taken back to base.

10th March: Two aircraft were sent on a sea search but after 8 hours they returned to base with no results.

11th March: Air Tests were carried out and fighter affiliation practice and local circuits and landings.

12th March: Thirteen Aircraft join a formation of 457 aircraft to bomb Essen. The centre of the bombing area was the giant Krupp factory just west of the Essen centre, with the later bombing drifting back to the north western outskirts. Krupp received 30 per cent more damage on that night than on the 5/6th March. Each aircraft was carrying various bombs and incendiaries and dropped from a height of around 16000/17000ft. Most aircraft were successful.

HE412 piloted by S/Ldr Macpherson had to turn back shortly after take-off owing to port engine trouble. He landed safely at base with his full bomb load.

HE167 piloted by Sgt Sneddon, at 21.21hrs over the target area, heard and felt a very large explosion, on inspection of the aircraft by the crew, it was revealed that a hole in the starboard wing about a foot across was seen. The aircraft carried on and finished the mission.

Map of Germany including major cities attacked in WW2 (Wikimedia Commons)

HE180 pilot Sgt Symes' oxygen supply failed and was compelled to return to base at 20.40hrs. He landed safely with full bomb load.

13th March: Today saw a return to gardening. Five aircraft took off for the 'Jellyfish,' area. The usual mines of 2x500lbs were carried and dropped from 600/700ft, all vegetables being planted successfully. Target identified again by Pointe du Toulinguet. All aircraft returned safely, apart from HE165 which had been hit by flak, but managed to make an emergency landing back at base.

14th March: Training flying day.

HE165 which made an emergency landing after being hit by flak.

15th March: P/O J.A. Hope was awarded the D.F.C. for his operation on Essen on the night of the 5th March. This was the first D.F.C. awarded to the squadron.

16th March: Flying training was carried out by new crews not yet operational.

17th March: No flying due to adverse weather conditions. Football matches were arranged for aircrews.

18th March: The squadron was informed at 10.30hrs that they were required for operations. At 13.30hrs the squadron was informed that the operation was abandoned.

19th March: The squadron was detailed for operations. The operations were cancelled at 21.00hrs.

20th March: The squadron was ready for operations. Weather was extremely poor so little flying was done. Operations were cancelled at 18.30hrs.

21st March: The squadron not needed for operations. Air tests and cross countries were carried out. Aircraft 'H' piloted by Sgt Greenfield developed a severe swing on take-off, hit a pile of gravel and crashed on the end of No. 4 runway. None of the crew were injured but the a/c was a write off.

22nd March: The squadron was detailed for operations at 10.00hrs. Local flying took place. At 17.00hrs operations were cancelled. No other flying due to bad weather.

23th March: Five aircraft detailed for a gardening sortie this time to the 'Nectarine' area. Aircraft took off from 19.20hrs onwards, all carrying 1500lb mines which were dropped from 800ft. Four of the aircraft planted their vegetables successfully.

HE167 ZO-A, took off at 19.22hrs and nothing further was heard. The aircraft, piloted by Sgt Duckmanton, had actually come down near the Terschelling Islands, it had blown up on hitting the sea, the cause unknown.

The crew of HE167 was: Pilot: Sgt. Henry Cavell Duckmanton, Navigator: Sgt. Douglas Robert Jeffrey, Bomb Aimer: Sgt. Basil John France Crook, Wireless Operator: Sgt. Samuel Robert Outra Hermon. All the above were killed in the crash. Air Gunner: Sgt E.W. Booth survived the crash and despite his injuries swam ashore. He was captured and became a Prisoner of War (POW). The airmen who lost their lives that night are buried in the West Terschelling General Cemetery, Terschelling Friesland, Netherlands.

The graves of the crew of Wellington HE167 code ZO-A, who lost their lives on the 23/3/43 on a gardening trip to the Friesans. They are buried in the west Terschelling General Cemetery, Friesland, Netherlands. Graves numbers 87,88,89,90

24th March: Thirteen aircraft were detailed for operations. Aircraft from previous night's operations returned from Holme and Pocklington. Operations were cancelled at 22.30hrs.

25th March: Squadron was stood down due to bad weather.

26th March: Fourteen aircraft joined a large force of 455 aircraft for a raid on Duisburg. All aircraft ran in to heavy cloud which meant pinpointing and bombing the area very difficult. All aircraft dropped their bombs except Wellington HE168 piloted by Sgt Fletcher. His navigator reported winds different from those forecasted, so he altered course approaching the Dutch coast. When approaching the target area, they encountered 10/10ths cloud making visibility impossible, also they ran in to heavy flak. The navigator informed the captain it would be impossible to pinpoint the target, so the captain decided to return to base. The bombs were jettisoned into the sea off the Dutch course from 18000ft.

27th March: The squadron were detailed for operations but were cancelled at 14.00hrs.

28th March: Two aircraft took off on a sea search at 10.00hrs. They returned to base three hours later with no result.

Also, 15 aircraft were detailed on a bombing raid to St. Nazaire in France as part of a big formation of 323 aircraft. The payload was various bombs and incendiaries dropped from around

14000/15000ft. All crews reported good visibility and little opposition in the form of light flak. All aircraft had successful trips with no incidents reported.

29th March: Eleven aircraft from the squadron joined a formation to bomb Bochum, the main force consisting of 149 Wellingtons. The aircrafts were carrying the usual load of mixed bombs and dropped from various heights of 14000/17000ft. Only 2 of the aircraft had straight forward trips. Wellingtons HE165, HE170, HE179, HE412 LN432 and MS490 were all hit by flak, some worse than others, but all the aircraft made it back to base but HE165 had to make an emergency landing.

HE395 piloted by P/O Eastwood was only half an hour into the sortie when the aircraft developed low oil pressure. The captain decided to return to base and jettisoned his load into the sea from 6000ft.

HE 385 ZO-M piloted by F/O E.R. Culf was recorded in the ORBs as missing. In fact, the aircraft was over Holland when it was attacked by a Messerschmitt 110 night fighter flown by Oberleutnant August Geiger and crashed at Zwiep (Gelderland) 2Km east of Barchem and 4Km south/south east of Lochem, Holland.

F/O Leslie Duncan McAlister.

The crew of HE385 was Pilot: F/O Edward Richard Culff, Navigator: Sgt. Thomas Albert Dew, Bomb Aimer: F/O Leslie Duncan McAllister, Wireless Operator: Sgt. Albert Charles August Veeck, Air Gunner: Sgt. Hubert Roy Wilmore, all were RAFVR and were buried in Larem (Barchem) General Cemetery, Gelderland, Netherlands.

HE548 Piloted by Sgt A. Lucas took off at 19.44hrs on the raid to Bochum, the ORBs reported nothing else heard from aircraft so presumed missing.

The crew of HE548 was: Pilot: Sgt. Arthur Lucas, Navigator: F/O. Kenneth Flaxman Smart, Bomb Aimer Sgt Arthur William Earnest Wilson, W/Op: F/Sgt Hugh Garfield Allen, Air Gunner: Sgt. Denys Andrew.

Very little is known about the crash apart from the aircraft was another casualty at the hands of August Geiger, the second kill of that night for Geiger, and the aircraft presumably crashed into the North Sea. Pilot Sgt Lucas' usual navigator had been taken ill on an operation on the 26/27th February and was substituted by a number of navigators before F/O Smart took the roll on that night, unfortunately to be his last.

30th March: The squadron was stood down.

31st March: Wing Commander A.G Duguid took over as Commander of the squadron from W/C Waterhouse.

The month of March saw the squadron undertake 97 sorties with a loss of 3 aircraft, Wellingtons HE167, HE385 and HE 548 and 14 aircrew, and one being taken as a POW. Another aircraft HE181 was lost on the 21st March due to a flying accident.

F/O Kenneth Flaxman Smart

Mick Dillon was born in India from New Zealand parents. He joined the New Zealand Air Force and trained as an air gunner. In November 1942 he joined 196 Squadron. He conducted a full tour, bombing targets such as Cologne, Wilhelmshaven, Hamburg, Essen, Stuttgart, Manheim, and Dusseldorf, also his crew also bombed the U-boat pens at St. Nazaire and did mine laying at Lorient and Brest. On the 16th June 1943 he was commissioned, promoting him to the rank of Pilot Officer. He completed his tour of 29 raids before being transferred to No. 83 O.T.U. on the 17th July 1943. Mick was then transferred back on to Operations with 103 Squadron on Lancasters. On his 37th sortie in April 1944 he and his crew set off on a raid to France. When returning, their aircraft was hit by flak and crashed in flames near Meharicourt. Four of his crew bailed out successfully but Mick and 2 other of the air gunners were unable to get out of the burning plane and died in the crash. They were buried in Meharicourt. Mick was 26 when he died.

April 1943

1st April: Aircrew attended an International Film Show at Station Headquarters.

2nd April: Air Tests, local flying, cross country and circuits and landings were carried out.

3rd April: Three aircraft were detailed for gardening in the 'Jellyfish' area near Brest. Two of the aircraft planted the vegetables successfully from 700ft. On their returned they landed at RAF Topcliffe near Thirsk. Wellington HE180, piloted by Sgt Swain, developed engine trouble and abandoned the mission and returned home landing at RAF Weston.

4th April: Wing Commander Waterhouse was taken off the strength of the squadron being appointed the Commander of the Station and promoted to the rank of Group Captain.

Three aircraft were detailed on a sea search, but after around 5hrs of searching they found nothing.

Ten aircraft set off as part of a formation to bomb Kiel. All aircraft carrying various bombs and incendiaries and to be dropped from around 17000ft. The aircraft ran in to 10/10ths cloud which obscured the target. All aircraft reported dropping their bombs towards a glow beneath the cloud, and the raid turned out to be a failure. Of the ten aircraft, one, when proceeding to take off, had a burst tyre so was unable to take off.

HE166 piloted by Sgt Temlett returned after 15 minutes owing to the port wing being low, which would not trim. In addition, the rear gunner's clear vision panel was stuck. While trying to free it, rear gunner Sgt Marshall's oxygen tube was carried away. The pilot therefore returned to base and missed the trip.

5th April: Six aircraft took off on a sea search, but after several hours of searching, returned to base with no results.

6th April: Air to sea firing and air bombing training took place.

7th April: Stand down due to bad weather.

8th April: Six aircraft detailed to bomb Duisburg. Two off the aircraft were unable to take off owing to the short runway to be used. Of the other four, two dropped their bombs although the target was covered with 10/10ths cloud. Both attacks were not very reliable.

HE168 piloted by Sgt Hitchins did not attack the target as Gee (radar) was u/s, and also, was unable to maintain the aircraft height so returned to base and jettisoned his load on the way.

HE170 piloted by Sgt McBain failed to attack the target owing to complete absence of P.F.F. (Path Finder Force), and the cloud cover. Bombs were brought back to base.

9th April: Air bombing and air gunnery practice.

10th April: Ten aircraft were detailed for bombing of Frankfurt. One aircraft failed to take off owing to a petrol leak in one of the wings. The other 9 aircraft encountered bad visibility over the target area due to 10/10ths cloud. The various bombs and incendiaries were dropped from around 16000ft. Two aircraft, on return, landed at other bases, one at RAF Tangmere and one at RAF Abingdon.

11th April: Four aircraft set off on a gardening operation in the 'Nectarine' area. All aircraft successfully planted their mines and returned to base.

12th April: No flying. Organised sports in the afternoon.

13th April: Some crews visited the Air Sea Rescue Service at Bridlington.

14th April: Eleven aircraft detailed for a bombing mission to Stuttgart. One aircraft failed to take off due to an electrical earth trouble. All aircraft were carrying various bombs and incendiaries and were dropped from around 16000ft. Six of the aircraft were successful, and on return, landed at RAF Beaulieu in Hampshire.

HE168 piloted by Sgt Rhoades decided to return to base owing to starboard engine trouble after reaching the Thames Estuary.

HE220 piloted by S/Ldr Macpherson returned to base as an overlord tank cock was wired up. Second pilot operated the wrong cock. Both engines cut three times, so the pilot decided to return at 21.33hrs after reaching Lincoln.

HE166 landed at RAF Tangmere after the raid. The aircraft took off again to return to base. On take-off one of the engines cut on HE166, and the aircraft crashed killing all on board.

The crew was: Pilot: Sgt Russell Verran Rosser DFM, Bomb Aimer: Sgt John Reginald Gallimore Calvert, Wireless Operator: Sgt Denis Charles Grocock, Navigator: Sgt Phillip Joseph Conwell, Air Gunner: Sgt Herbert Wilcock. Russell V. Rosser was buried in Pontyates (St.Mary) churchyard, Pontyates, Carmarthen. Wales. John R.G. Calvert and Denis C. Grocock was buried in Tangmere (St. Andrew) Churchyard, Chichester. Herbert Wilcock was buried at Lancaster Cemetery, Lancaster. Lancashire.

Sgt Russell V. Rosser DFM

Pilot Russell Rosser was seen as a bit of a hero in his hometown. It was reported in his local paper in Wales, that on one occasion, Russell's aircraft was attacked over the North Sea by an Me109, the aircraft was hit and with one of the engines on fire he put the aircraft in to a corkscrew dive to put it out, at the same time his rear gunner shot down the enemy aircraft.

15th April: Aircraft from previous night's raid returned to base.

Sgt Herbert Wilcock

16th April: Three aircraft went on a sea search but returned to base with no results.

Fourteen aircraft from the squadron joined a force to bomb Mannheim. All aircraft were carrying 6x500lb bombs and dropped from around 15000ft.

Nine aircraft were successful and returned with no incidents.

HE178 piloted by W/O Stead decided to return at 21.50hrs owing to unsatisfactory state of one of his starboard engines, also Gee and D.R.C. u/s.

HE398 piloted by Sgt Dyson decided to return as the port air intake strut was broken but landed safely at 21.50 with full bomb load.

HE162 piloted by Sgt Temlett, when over target area, ran in to searchlights and accurate heavy flak. His aircraft was hit and sustained tail damage but made a safe return.

HE 469 piloted by W/Cdr. Duguid successfully completed their mission and were returning to base. As the aircraft crossed the English coast it ran out of petrol, the pilot turned the aircraft to head for the sea and all the crew baled out safely, the aircraft crashing into the sea.

HE387 ZO-Z Piloted by Sgt Morgan took off at 21.09hrs but nothing else was heard from them again. It emerged that HE387 crashed near Couvron et Aumencourt, France.

HE387 was shot down by night fighter pilot Hauptmann Hans-Karl Kamp of the 7. /NJG 4, flying a Bf 110 or Do 217 from Juvincourt airfield. Also claimed by light flak unit 1. /leichte Flak-Abteilung 773 (v). The flak claim was rejected, the victory for Hauptmann Kamp confirmed.

The crew was: Pilot: P/O Ivor Malcolm Payne Morgan, Navigator: F/Sgt Roy Hill, Bomb Aimer: P/O Albert William Arnold Trevarthen, Wireless Operator: Sgt Norman Bruce, Air Gunner: Sgt Leslie Pickford. The crew of the aircraft were all buried in The Couvron et Aumencourt Communal Cemetery, Aisne, France

17th April: Three aircraft were detailed for a gardening mission in the 'Jellyfish' area. One aircraft was unable to take off owing to the intercommunications being u/s. The other two aircraft planted their mines successfully and returned to base.

18th April: Flight training carried out. The C/O, W/Cmdr A.G. Duguid was admitted to sick quarters with a sprained ankle as a result of a parachute descent on the 16th April. S/Ldr N. Alexander took over command of the squadron.

19th April: Ten aircraft detailed for operations, but these were cancelled at 18.00hrs. W/Cmdr Duguid returned to duty from S.S.Q.

20th April: Air training. Another visit to the A.S.R.S at Bridlington.

21st April: Three aircraft went on a sea search but after four hours they returned to base with no results. S/Ldr Alexander assumed command of the squadron while W/Cmdr Duguid attended a course of instruction on engine handling.

22nd April: Three aircraft set off on a gardening operation to the 'Jellyfish' area. All aircraft was successful but landed at RAF Pershore, Worcestershire on the return. Organised sports in the afternoon. S/Ldr Macpherson assumed command of the Squadron as S/Ldr Alexander was on leave.

23rd April: Stand down due to bad weather.

24th April: W/Cmdr Duguid resumed command of the squadron. Fifteen aircraft were detailed for operations but were cancelled at 18.00hrs.

The graves of the crew of HE387

25th April: A large number of the aircrew attended a service at the Church in Leconfield Village for Easter Sunday.

26th April: Fourteen aircraft were detailed for a raid on Duisburg, but one failed to take off. All the aircraft were carrying various bombs and incendiaries and were dropped from around 17000ft., ten of the aircraft had successful trips and returned to base.

HE171 piloted by F/O Blythe had reached Cottesmore when the aircraft generator packed up, so the pilot returned to base and landed safely with the full bomb load.

MS491 piloted by P/O Mallinson developed engine trouble due to the TR9 and constant speed indicator becoming u/s. The aircraft crash landed at 05.15hrs at Hazel Grove, New Waltham three miles south of Grimsby. No injuries to the crew were reported, but the aircraft was a write-off.

HE168 Piloted by Sgt Fletcher failed to return. It was shot down by night fighter pilot Hauptmann Hans-Dieter Frank of the 2. /NJG 1, flying a Bf 110 G-4 from Gilze-Rijen airfield.

The crew was: Pilot: Sgt George Frederick Fletcher, Navigator: Sgt Ernest George Francis, Bomb Aimer: Sgt Eric Thomas Dunn Hardee, Air Gunner: Sgt James Alfred Hawkins. Wireless Operator: Frank Theodore Pratt.

Wellington HE168, was airborne at 00.01 hrs on Easter Monday the 27th April, and was shot down on its way back from the raid on Duisburg by a night fighter at 03.15 hrs. It crashed in the plots 'Hekke Poel', arable land, and 'De Drie Morgen', pasture, in the polder of Munnikenland at the village of Poederoijen in the Dutch Province of Gelderland which lies about 10 km south-east of Gorinchem, on the Breda – Utrecht Road, Holland.

The residents of Poederoijen reported that on the night of 26/27th April 1943, the town was struck by a terrifying noise. Those who looked up saw a burning plane in the sky crashing in the polder of Munnikenland. The patrolman of Poederoijen (W.A. van Giessen) called Mayor Pos of the municipality of Brakel (This area is now part of the municipality of Zaltbommel). Together with the local doctor, C. van Steenis, they went to the plane.

On arrival, they found four persons of the Deutsche Wehrmacht (Defence Force) from Gorinchem, who had seen the plane crash, already there. The Germans guarded the plane and the area around, so that no one could escape from it, but also to stop any enthusiastic bystanders getting too close to the burning remains and hurting themselves.

The Mayor of Poederoijen reported that, at the crash site in the meadow, they initially found three persons severely burned inside the remains of the aircraft and one person, probably the pilot, Sgt. Fletcher, outside adjacent to the burning plane. One was identified by his name on his coat and the others were being buried as 'onbekende personen' (unidentified persons). It was initially a mystery as to what had happened to the fifth crew member who could possibly have baled out, causing heightened security at the ferry ports in the region. The missing air-gunner, Sgt. Hawkins, could well have tried to leave his cockpit just before the plane crashed, for he was later soon found dead in a field nearby to the village.

The Deutsche Wehrmacht did a careful investigation about the bomber, and the commander of the Gilze Rijen airport made the decision to bury the bodies of the five deceased RAF aircrew at the cemetery of Poederoijen, in a dedicated grave near to the small church, in this quiet town between the rivers Maas and Waal, in a beautiful resting place, but inevitably far away from their homes, wives and parents.

The funeral was held on 30th April 1943, with a burial service at 15.00 hrs, in the Poederoijen Protestant Churchyard, of which only Fletcher and Hawkins were identified, the coffins being carried by six members of the Air Protection Service into a communal grave. The German authorities could not be present to provide military honours because there were difficulties for them, possibly even a general strike on that day, with so many people staying at home to listen to their radios to hear the latest news from London. The advice that came through was, refuse to go, and if needed, to hide. Then the strike started. The Germans had their hands full to stop the strike. For this reason, the German Wehrmacht informed the mayor that they could not be present at the funeral.

A noticeably big crowd from Poederoijen and other close villages gathered in the graveyard. In deep silence the coffins, covered in black sheets, were let down into the hole.

Three photos of George Francis, the last one with his cousin, Roy Andrews, who was killed in 1941 flying in a Fairey Swordfish. Roy was in the Fleet Air Arm.

27th April: Fourteen aircraft detailed for operation but was later cancelled.

28th April: Six aircraft was detailed for a gardening operation in the Forget Me Nots area. Two aircraft completed the mission, but HE162 piloted by W/O Mellor, encountered cloud and heavy rain and was unable to pinpoint the target, so returned home jettisoning the mines over the sea.

HE170 piloted by Sgt Swain had completed the mission and planted the mines and on the return was shot down.

The crew was: Pilot: Sgt Frederick Charles Swain, Navigator: Sgt Albert Wheatley, Bomb Aimer: Sgt Edward George Quick, Wireless Operator: Sgt George Richard Burgess, Air Gunner: Sgt Edwin Donald Curling.

HE170 was attacked by a German Bf 110 night fighter while flying over the southern part of Jylland. The pilot of the night fighter was Oberleutnant Meess of 6. /NJG 3 who with his

A memorial was placed at the site of HE170s crash

Bordfunker Unteroffizier Ostheimer (gunner), were led to the target by the radar station 'Amiese' located at Barsmark om Løjtland.

A fire started in the Wellington and the pilot tried at 00:57 hours to do a belly landing near Bjerndrup northeast of Løgumkloster. The aircraft had skidded approximately 1500 ft. when it hit a drainage canal. The Wellington turned over on its back and a fierce fire started. At 01:15 air gunner Sgt Edwin D. Curling and navigator Sgt Albert Wheatley were found 30 ft. east of the canal, both severely injured and were taken to Tønder hospital. They both died on the very same day, Wheatley at 13.15hrs and Curling at 13.18hrs. At 07:00 hours, bomb aimer Sgt Edward G. Quick was found dead in the canal underneath an engine and was brought to the Tønder hospital. In the morning one body was found standing on its head in the canal and one was found floating in the water. They were wireless operator Sgt George R. Burgess and pilot Sgt Frederick C. Swain. The whole crew was laid to rest in Aabenraa Cemetery on the 7th May 1943.

Sgt Reginald Harry Taylor

Another report read:

When the mission was done the plane came under fire over Løgumkloster. Young people on their way home from a meeting in Løgumgårde were able to tell about a heavy air battle towards Arrild. The tail of the plane was burning, and it turned towards Agerskov. Shortly after it returned from Agerskov, flying over Branderup, the duel between the English plane and the German fighter still went on. Everyone realised that the Wellington was going to make an emergency landing. It swept down just east of the farms in Bjerndrup, unluckily the slide ended in a canal, where the plane tipped over and ended up on the edge. The time was now around 00.50. The result was an exploding fire with tall flames, which could be seen far away.

A number of spectators arrived on the spot, situated about 450 ft. from the road and the farm of August Petersen. The police and local residents tried to save the crew because they could hear wailing. The area was closed off and the families living nearby were evacuated because of the danger of exploding bombs. Two survivors were taken to the hospital in Tønder, where they passed away shortly after each other around 13.15 the following day. When the dawn broke the remaining 3 crew members were found. They were taken to the chapel of Løgumkloster Hospital. Before noon, the pilot who had shot the plane down at Bjerndrup, arrived in a small sports plane. He was photographed by the wreckage. Some days later the burned out plane was removed.

HE220 piloted by Sgt Atkins is believed to have been shot down by flak, the multi barrel flak batteries were very active in the area that night. Coned in searchlights of the Marine Flak-Abteilung

Batteries, the aircraft was hit by light and heavy flak and exploded and crashed in Eckernforde Bay, Baltic Sea

The crew was: Pilot: Sgt John Frederick Atkins, Navigator: Sgt Frank Guy, Bomb Aimer: Sgt Reginald Harry Taylor, Wireless Operator: Sgt William McDonough, Air Gunner: Sgt Patrick William John Morrow. The aircraft was lost without trace and the crew are remembered on The Runnymede Memorial.

HE395 Piloted by F/Lt. Bonard was the third aircraft to be lost on that night.

The crew was: Pilot: F/Lt. Ian Numa Bonard. Navigator: F/O John Joseph Wilfred Burns. Bomb Aimer: P/O Albert Robert Potter. Wireless Operator: P/O Basil Arthur Curtis. Air Gunner: P/O John Ireland Pearson Ford.

Returning towards the west over Denmark from the target area, HE395 was again picked up on radar by 'Amiese' the radar on Løjtland. Lieutenant Meess was again the German night fighter pilot who attacked the aircraft. HE395 caught fire and crashed at 00:15 in a field 1500 ft. south of Over Jersdal and broke up and was completely burned out. HE170 and HE395 were the only two aircraft shot down in WWII by Lieutenant Ernst Meess. A monument was erected in memory of the crew of HE395 by Danish veterans of WW I in the parish of Vedstedand, unveiled on 5 May, 1949.

29th April: Three aircraft went out on a sea search, but after six hours returned with no results.

30th April: The squadron stood by for operations, but these were cancelled at 12.00hrs. No other flying due to bad weather.

This brought to an end, operations for April 1943. The squadron had flown 103 sorties. April was by far the costliest of the war so far. The squadron had lost eight aircraft, HE166, HE168, HE170, HE220, HE387 and HE395 with the loss of all their crews, 30 men in all. The other two aircraft HE469 ran out of petrol and MS491 due to engine trouble.

Left and above. Two photos of the monument erected in memory of the crew of HE395 by Danish veterans of WWI in the parish of Vedstedand unveiled on the 5th May 1949

May 1943

1st May: A lecture was given by Lt. Hayden, a naval officer, on submarine warfare. Two aircrews took part in a 'Wings for Victory', parade at Driffield.

2nd May: Eleven aircraft were detailed for operations to bomb Duisburg, but the operation was cancelled at 21.45hrs.

3rd May: Twelve aircraft detailed for operations but were cancelled just before briefing.

4th May: Thirteen aircraft were detailed to take part in a bombing raid on Dortmund. This was the first major raid on Dortmund. Once again, the squadron was on their way back to The Ruhr, which was referred to by all aircrew as 'Happy Valley'. The squadron was part of a force of 596 aircraft of all the Bomber Command Groups to attack the city that night. All aircraft carried high explosive and incendiary bombs and dropped from around 19000ft, nine aircraft completed the mission with no complications.

HE412 piloted by Sgt Temlett was hit by the heavy flak over the target area and sustained a large hole in the port fuselage near the tail, thankfully none of the crew were injured, they returned safely base to base.

Wellington LN432 was piloted by Sgt Watson, when the aircraft should have been 35 miles from Tekel, two cones of about 6/12 searchlights were seen to port and starboard and also light and heavy flak, the navigator decided he was lost so the pilot decided to return and jettisoned his bomb load. After landing back at base a major oil leak was discovered.

HE398 piloted by Sgt Sneddon had to return early owing to guns in the rear turret not staying cocked. All bombs were brought back.

HE162 took off at 22.52hrs and nothing else was heard of from the aircraft, and it was declared missing.

The crew was, Pilot: Sergeant. John Staniforth, Navigator: Sergeant. Harry George Graham. Bomb Aimer: Sergeant. Ronald William Lynn, Wireless Operator: Sergeant George William Challoner James. Air Gunner: Sergeant Bertie Edward Taylor.

The aircraft crashed near Gelsenkirchen, but nothing more is known about the crash. All the crew are buried in Reichswald Forest War Cemetery.

5th May: Two aircraft was detailed for a sea search but was then cancelled. Aircraft from previous night's raid that landed away from base returned.

6th May: S/Ldr Alexander assumed command of the squadron as W/Cdr Duguid proceeded on leave.

7th May: Four aircraft were detailed for minelaying but was cancelled at 18.00hrs. One aircraft crash landed away from base at Grove, the crew was uninjured.

8th May: Stand down due to bad weather.

9th May: S/Ldr Alexander in the capacity of Commanding Officer attended A.O.C.s conference at H.Q. No. 4 Group. Fourteen aircraft detailed for raid on Duisburg but was cancelled at 22.00hrs.

10th May: No flying, weather u/s.

11th May: Twelve aircraft detailed for raid on Duisburg, again cancelled at 20.00hrs.

12th May: Twelve aircraft was detailed to bomb Duisburg. All aircraft was carrying high explosive bombs and incendiaries and dropped from about 18000ft., ten aircraft returned after successful trips.

HZ362 Piloted by P/O Mallinson returned early owing to Gee and wireless failure. All bombs were brought back.

HE398 piloted by Sgt Greenfield took off at 22.52, and nothing was heard from the pilot again and was declared missing.

It later emerged that HE398 was shot down by night fighter pilot Lieutenant Robert Denzel of the 12./NJG 1, flying Bf 110 G-4 G9+HZ from Bergen airfield, and crashed into the North Sea 30 km west of Callantsoog, Holland, without trace.

The crew was: Pilot: F/Sgt. Jack Greenfield, Navigator: F/Sgt. Robert Burridge, Bomb Aimer: Sgt. William O'Neill, Wireless Operator: Sgt. Kenneth Foster Bell, Air Gunner: Sgt William Eddington. All are remembered on the Runnymede memorial.

13th May: Eleven aircraft of the squadron were detailed to bomb Bochum as part of a 442 strong raid. Positioned in almost the centre of the Ruhr' it was the regions fourth largest city. The payload was the usual mix of bombs and incendiaries and dropped from 18000ft. All aircraft were successful.

HZ362 Piloted by P/O Mallinson was hit by heavy flak immediately after leaving the target area, and sustained damage. The port inner rear petrol tank was holed and small holes in port and starboard wings and starboard side of fuselage was sustained. Thankfully, despite the damage none of the crew reported injury, it was a close thing. The damaged Wellington flew back to base where it made a safe landing. It was an excellent piece of piloting by the P/O Mallinson.

14th May: Aircrew given a stand down.

15th May: W/Cdr Duguid resumed command of the squadron.

A Vickers Wellington being bombed-up with a 4000lb Cookie.

16th May: Six aircraft set off on a gardening mission to the 'Artichoke' area. All was carrying 2x1500 mines. Five aircraft planted the vegetables successfully, but HE178 piloted by Sgt Watson was unable to pinpoint the target so returned to base with the mines.

17th May: Aircraft from previous night's operation arrived back at base after landing at St. Eval.

18th May: Fairly intense air training was carried out.

19th May: Six aircraft was detailed for gardening operations but was cancelled at 18.00hrs.

20th May: W/Cmdr Duguid, C/O of the squadron, was appointed Officer Commanding R.A.F. Station Leconfield during the absence of the C/O who was on leave.

21st May: Four aircraft were detailed for gardening in the 'Nectarine' area. All aircraft was successful and returned to base.

22nd May: S/Ldr Macpherson and F/Ltn Wilson were awarded the D.F.C. for operations with the squadron.

23rd May: Seventeen aircraft were detailed for a raid on Dortmund, but only sixteen took off due to illness in one of the crews. The squadrons' aircraft was part of a massive 826 aircraft to hit the city that night, dropping 2000 tons of bombs in just one hour. Fourteen aircraft dropped their bombs and returned safely.

HE142 piloted by Sgt Hitchins was badly hit by flak, one of the port propellers was splintered, the port wing was holed, and the port aileron cable was severed but the aircraft made it back to base safely.

MS496 piloted by W/O Mellor returned early owing to the port engine being u/s due to low oil pressure.

HE389 piloted by P/O Mallinson also returned early, owing to starboard engine trouble and low oil pressure.

24th May: Crews were stood down.

25th May: Three aircraft took off on a sea search but returned after several hours with no results.

Sixteen aircraft was detailed to bomb Dusseldorf. One aircraft failed to take off due to a faulty intercom. The other fifteen took off as part of a formation of 729 aircraft on the raid that night. Twelve aircraft bombed the target and returned successfully.

HE180 piloted by P/O McBain returned early, owing to the oil temperature in the starboard engine too high and the oil pressure too low.

HZ363 piloted by Sgt Norris returned early due to engine trouble, landing at Hardwick.

MS490 piloted by S/Ldr Alexander returned early owing to engine trouble, again with low oil pressure and high temperature.

26th May: W/Cmdr Duguid ceased from being Station Commander. Fifteen aircraft detailed for operations but were cancelled at 22.00hrs.

27th May: Nine aircraft took off to raid Essen as part of a formation of 518 aircraft. All aircraft had successful trips and returned to base. The only exception being MS490 piloted by S/Ldr Alexander, which was hit by heavy flak, but returned to base safely. Because of cloud on the night, it led to scattered bombing, damaging Essen and ten other towns.

28th May: Two aircraft set out on a sea search but with no results.

Three aircraft detailed on a gardening operation in the 'Nectarine' area. All aircraft successfully laid their mines and returned to base.

29th May: Thirteen aircraft was detailed to bomb Wuppertal as part of a 719 bomber raid. Eleven aircraft returned after completing the mission. One aircraft, HE901 piloted by F/O Mallinson, returned early due to the illness of the navigator.

HE362 was damaged by heavy flak but returned safely.

Wuppertal, being relatively close to the UK, saw maximum payloads being carried by all the aircraft. There was only light defence, and the bombing force was able to deliver their bombs accurately, the old town burned down when a firestorm took hold, five of the six major factories were destroyed and the homes of 100,000 people.

30th May: Crews were stood down.

31st May: Six aircraft detailed for mining but was cancelled at 17.00hrs

This brought to an end, operations for May. The squadron flew a total of 109 sorties in the month. Considering the losses from other squadrons, May had been a good month for 196, with the loss of only 2 aircraft, HE162 and HE398 and their crews, a total of 10 men.

No.196 Squadron, circa 1943.

June 1943

1st June: The squadron detailed six aircraft for gardening in the 'Artichoke' area. Four aircraft planted their vegetables and returned safely.

HE484 piloted by Sgt Hitchins believed that he obtained a pinpoint on the Estuary of Aven and Belon, but there was so much cloud that he could not confirm it and decided to bring the vegetables back.

HE163 piloted by F/O Deans took off but almost immediately, at about 2000ft, the starboard engine lost power and boost. The pilot made a circuit of the airfield, overshot the field and jettisoned the mines in an adjacent field, before crash landing a quarter of a mile North of Arram Grange. The crew escaped with no injuries, but the aircraft was completely burned out.

2nd June: Five aircraft set off on a mine-laying operation to the 'Artichoke' area for the second night running. All aircraft returned after a successful sortie.

3rd June: Two aircraft detailed to mine the Beeches area and returned successfully.

4th June: Eleven aircraft detailed for operations but was called off before briefing. A searchlight crew visited the squadron and were shown around by the Squadron Air Crew Officer – no aircraft being entered, or any secret equipment being seen by the visitors.

5th June: Formation of three aircraft with W/Cmdr Duguid as leader over Withernsea for 'Wings for Victory', week. Lecture given by Naval Officer Lieutenant Styles on 'Results of Gardening'.

6th June: Air tests were carried out.

7th June: Thirteen aircraft was detailed for operations but was cancelled at 21.45 hrs due to weather u/s.

8th June: Four aircraft detailed for gardening but cancelled at 18.00hrs.

W/Op: F/Sgt Stan Hurrell who was in HE163 when it crash landed and burnt out.

9th June: Fourteen aircraft detailed on operations to bomb Essen but was cancelled at 22.00 hrs due to bad weather.

10th June: Lecture on 'Escaping', to new crews by an Intelligence Officer from R.A.F. Driffield.

11th June: On a raid to Dusseldorf as part of a force of 783 aircraft, fifteen aircraft took off with various bomb loads and successfully bombed the target.

HE513 piloted by Sgt Dyson was hit by flak causing a hole in the cockpit but returned safely with no injuries.

HE901 piloted by F/Lt Wilson D.F.C. was also hit by heavy flak over the target area but returned safely.

MS486 ZO-R piloted by F/O Jackson dropped their 4000lb bomb and set course for home. The aircraft crashed at 2.20hrs near Stanhoe near Bircham Newton, Norfolk. The pilot and navigator P/O Lea were killed. The rest of the crew was severely injured and taken to Ely Hospital.

The narrative that follows is by the rear gunner Ivor Prothero written around 1975.

RAF Leconfield, East Yorks. 11 June 1943:

"The afternoon and evening at Leconfield, base of 196 Squadron, was fairly overcast with almost continuous rain. Crews awaited whilst a secondary take off time was arranged, eventually set for 23.00 hrs. We had a fairly rough take off, having run into what we thought to be runway water puddles causing us to skew to the runway edge before lift-off. Also, concern was expressed over the intercom that the under cart may have been lifted too early (possible damage?). This 'R' Roger Wellington X, was a new replacement aircraft which we had all tested several days before and the skipper's remarks were mainly that he found the controls stiff. By coincidence, a week or so before, whilst at flying control I saw the aircraft land, flown direct from the manufacturer's by a ferry pilot. It was of particular interest because it was noticed that it had no squadron lettering on its side when taxiing. To all of us watching, we were very surprised to see a sole figure of a rather slight lady, carrying a sizeable black bag, emerge. Very soon afterwards an Anson aircraft landed and picked her up where she presumably joined other ferry pilots.

We didn't seem to stick to any particular aircraft, although we had previously used 'Q' Queen for two or three Ruhr trips. This 'R' Roger was allotted to us and for the first operational trip to Dusseldorf it was to carry our first 4000lbs bomb. We all took a good look at it before boarding, agreeing that it looked large and ugly slung beneath the fuselage. Well before reaching the Dutch coast and still climbing, the port motor's high temperature reading was causing concern. So eventually it was decided to reduce speed and rate of climb. This would have resulted in putting us behind the scheduled bombing time over the target. To aid the situation it was decided to cut across one of our 'dog legs' of the planned route. Having altered course, we were at about 12,000ft in 10/10th cloud and most probably crossing the Dutch coast when there were three distinct A/A bursts, (probably from a flak ship), firstly lighting up the cloud beneath us, the second above, the third shook the aircraft and the starboard motor soon burst into flames. Resulting almost immediate in to a spirally dive to port which delayed some of the urgent actions called for over the intercom "starboard motor fire extinguisher" feathering it's propeller, shutting off the fuel supply and urgent bomb release. The effect of 'G' force in the rear turret was so great that I couldn't even lift an arm, whilst over the intercom I heard them struggling to regain control. Had I been able to move and put my parachute on, I'm pretty certain I would have baled out, those moments seemed so final.

When the skipper managed to pull out of the dive he regained part control, as, for a while, the rudder had frozen up. Having lost some 6,000ft and at a higher temperature, it soon eased off. Fortunately no one was hurt, the fire was out, and the reported damage involved many electrical and hydraulic failures, and some problems with the main compass. With this unsettled compass condition, it became necessary to break radio silence and obtain an accurate 'fix/QDM' (magnetic course to steer to reach you).

We received three almost immediate replies from UK bases, thus enabling true compass headings, checks, and a return course. With increasing difficulties, all our skipper's undoubted skills and energy were now called for in keeping airborne and avoiding further temperature build of that port motor. Although in cloud, and owing to cross winds, in order to get back on course the turning of reciprocals didn't help maintain height or level flight. It also became necessary to monitor and balance fuel supply from wing tanks, which became critical at one time. The possibilities of ditching were discussed briefly but none of us suggested any positive action. For example, lightening the aircraft by getting rid of heavy equipment etc. Some way out on approaching the Norfolk coast, and through radio contact with RAF Docking, we were informed that we were being diverted to nearby Bircham Newton airfield Norfolk. On route they had three searchlights coned at cloud base of 2000feet, which we found without much delay. About this time the skipper told us over the intercom that he intended to land the aircraft but added it would be a rough landing without the undercarriage (no hydraulics). He reminded us all that as we broke cloud the last chance at 2000 feet to bale out would have to be taken without delay. All replied that we would stay, with the usual comment, "that you can't take it back (the Chute) to the stores and change it when it doesn't open." Soon after breaking cloud, with the port wing slightly down from my turret, I had a glimpse of the well-lit runway and chance lights. Whilst the skipper was in contact with flying control on r/t, I may not have heard all that was said, but there seemed to be a question about 'call sign' procedure. However, he made it clear that he intended to come straight in, and not circuit. He then told us all to get to our crash positions. In my case, turret to beam, and I had time to put my 'chute at head height, in front of the guns. I believe procedure for the rest of the crew in getting to their respective positions, includes disconnecting their intercom. As I had mine still connected, I assume I was possibly the last in contact with the skipper, as he suddenly called, "can anyone see the lights?" Looking quickly now to my some-what limited side view and beneath us, I reported likewise, "no sign of any lights now". As there was no answer from anyone else I assumed that now at their crash positions, they were no longer on intercom. I'm fairly certain that firstly some rapid 'Call Sign', procedure was used by the skipper to flying control. His final message to them was clear. "Put your lights on, what are you trying to do, kill us all?" I believe then, that he must have opened up the throttle of the port motor, with the possibility of doing a circuit. With his intercom still switched on I heard him say, "Sorry chaps, crash".

Almost immediately sparks and flames passed the turret from the port motor and wing area. Bracing myself in the turret for the inevitable – I fancy the port wing hit first. Regaining consciousness somewhere in a fire near the starboard wing, confirmed later to be in a barley crop field some 3 feet high, I found it best to roll to the right and away from the fire. Experiencing considerable breathing difficulties and right arm and shoulder problems, but my legs seemed to be OK. Slight problems getting away from my Mae West which was on fire, stumbling, I managed to undo the tapes with my left hand and also pressed the harness quick release. At this stage, probably gathering my senses, thoughts of self-preservation must have taken over and get away from the fire. Wherever I turned there seemed to be a fairly strong cool wind blowing in my face, this later turned out to be smarting, effects of burns to hands and face. A week or so earlier we had been issued with whistles, which we were advised to attach to the top part of our battle dress blouse, so that in the event of ditching in the sea at any time, they could be an aid to contacting each other. On hearing a whistle I stopped and managed a short blow before it stuck in my mouth, which just increased my breathing difficulties. Having sensed the direction and realising someone else was about, I edged my way round the head of the blazing wreck where I could clearly see someone, Syd Mortimer our wireless operator was alongside a hedgerow. After our brief words and recognition he asked me if I could do anything with his leg, he was in a half sitting position with one leg almost wrapped round the other. I was briefly explaining that my right arm seemed useless and that my hands had deep cuts but were not bleeding (as seen in the light of the fire), when we heard Jack Atherton our bomber aimer calling (obviously delirious) at a point nearer to the fire, but not too far away. When I got to him, a broken loop of his parachute harness enabled me to use my left hand and pull him to one side a little way. He was pretty well alight. I must have passed out for a while, as the next thing I remember was a civilian bending over me, later confirmed to be a Mr Seaman the local ARP warden who I learned was first on the scene. I'm fairly certain that I said there were still two of our crew to find (pilot and navigator) and that the crackling sounds were probably small arms ammunition exploding and assured him before he left, that there was no bomb on board. Soon afterwards, I got this crazy idea that by walking beyond the fire area it might be possible to get some help. In attempting to get over an iron fence, half way over, I became stuck with insufficient strength to lift a second leg over, but I was soon rescued by the now advancing RAF ambulance crew.

We three survivors (wireless operator, bomber aimer, and I, rear gunner) were immediately taken to Bircham Newton RAF medical centre and then, transferred to RAF Hospital Ely, where for several months we received excellent treatment for various orthopaedic needs and first and second degree burns. In due course we were informed of the regrettable and upsetting news that both our skipper Frank Jackson and navigator Ron Lea had not survived the crash. Our skipper, Pilot Officer Frank Jackson gave his life trying to save us and the aircraft, he never saw his 21st birthday, a courageous and brave young man which we had the honour to serve under. For example, having just regained some control of the aircraft and before ordering 'bomb jettisoning', he said that we ought to continue to target, but we jointly voiced opinions against such an idea, thus we headed back to the UK. We never got to know the true circumstances of just why the runway lights were extinguished on that final approach. Unofficially we heard that there had been 'intruder' enemy aircraft in the area a night or so before."

The pilot of the aircraft, F/O Frank Jackson is buried in New Hunstanton Cemetery, Norfolk. (9 Miles from the crash site).

The navigator F/O Ronald Lea is buried in the War Graves plot at St. Mary's Church, Great Bircham. Norfolk. (4 Miles from crash site).

Ivor Prothero continues:

RAF Hospital, Ely- Burns Ward:

"Some ten days or so later, my bed was wheeled from the burns ward to the orthopaedic end, where Syd Mortimer (wireless operator) and Jack Atherton (bomb aimer) were receiving additional treatment for their serious leg injuries. I believe some of the body burns needed skin grafting also. Jack was not at all well and didn't talk then. However Syd and I had a good update on each other's condition and exchanged thoughts and memories which matched surprisingly well, in spite of some lost periods of time. The day and night care and attention given to us in the burns ward by the nursing staff was obviously superb, not forgetting those visiting ladies who basically wrote letters for us etc. Looking back regretfully, time and circumstances never allowed adequate thanks and appreciation to be expressed, before progressing onto convalescence elsewhere. Early on surprise ward visits, including some officers from Leconfield (196 Squadron), followed during July by some of our own ground crew staff, with their remarkable news that the squadron had been posted to nearby Witchford and were to convert onto Stirling Bombers. Whilst all war time air crews were volunteers, for one reason or another, none of us three survivors returned to operational flying.

One of my early surprises was to find myself alongside a squadron leader. He was a pilot, badly burned when his Stirling crashed into the Epsom Grandstands. One morning he was particularly annoyed at himself, somehow having allowed one of those self-closing rubber ward doors to spring back and damage his latest hand skin grafting. These rubber doors enabled us to keep hands chest high (avoiding downward blood pressure) and the use of one's elbows to open doors. A procedure I was to use later on. Strict privacy and total curtaining during the changing of dressings, and a complete absence of mirrors etc., never allowed us to see for example, how facial areas were healing. Ears were particularly uncomfortable, and a smile from a radio joke, regularly caused lips to bleed. Tommy Handley's radio show 'ITMA' and 'Mrs Mop - can I do you now, Sir?' was the highlight of the time. Eventually being informed that I had remarkable skin healing qualities, and having seen the photographs, I realised just how lucky I had been. Strange looking back now, but we were actually issued with packets of cigarettes almost daily and my bedside locker became well stocked up for me later on.

The confidence in the aircraft and in each other as crew members grew with experience and most probably at times gave us a false picture of ourselves. Although mainly defensive, the considerable fire power from the rear turret, having four Browning's, each gun capable of firing some 750 rounds per minute, harmonised for night firing. The 303 ammunition being fed through a lengthy gravity assisted feeder system, were made up of 1 in 4 tracer, armour piercing, incendiary, and ball rounds.

Going out, it was somewhat comforting to see many other types of aircraft at odd heights on the heading, until fading light reduced clarity. From then on, the increased risk of collisions and avoiding getting in the slipstream of some four engine aircraft ahead, kept us all alert.

Friendly fire, yes, on one occasion returning from the Ruhr, somewhere over Belgium, a Halifax mid-upper gunner let off a few rounds in our direction, just to let us know he didn't want us any nearer. We had seen him, against cloud gaining on us, slightly higher on our starboard side. Our own explanation was that some while before, unofficially, we had heard of captured Wellingtons, having been seen with guns firing from additional beam and nose positions over enemy territory. When in fact at that time the RAF were only using the rear gun positioned turrets. Additionally,

Flying Officer Frank Jackson photographed doing his training. Frank was reported to being a very extremely popular fellow who was a good sportsman. Prior to his training Frank was captain of Beaumont College, Old Windsor in 1938, then studied medicine at Trinity College, Cambridge.

about this time, Wellingtons were being withdrawn from main force bombers and replaced by four engine aircraft."

12th June: Six aircraft were detailed for gardening, two in the Lorient area and four to the St. Nazaire area. All aircraft were successful and returned to base with no incidents.

13th June: Two aircraft took off on a sea search but returned with no results.

14th June: Four aircraft again took off on a sea search but again returned with no results.

Four aircraft was detailed for gardening in the Beeches area. One aircraft landed at Bruntingthorpe in Leicester with problems and never proceeded. The other three aircraft was successful.

HE165 piloted by F/Lt Ellis was hit and extremely damaged by light flak from an enemy convoy. The aircraft returned to base but crash landed with damage to the aircraft, but the crew was uninjured. This was the second time HE165 had been hit by flak and crashed back at base

15th June: Air tests carried out.

16th June: Fighter affiliation and bombing practice carried out

17th June: Three aircraft carried out exercise 'Bullseye', one aircraft landed away from base after completing the exercise.

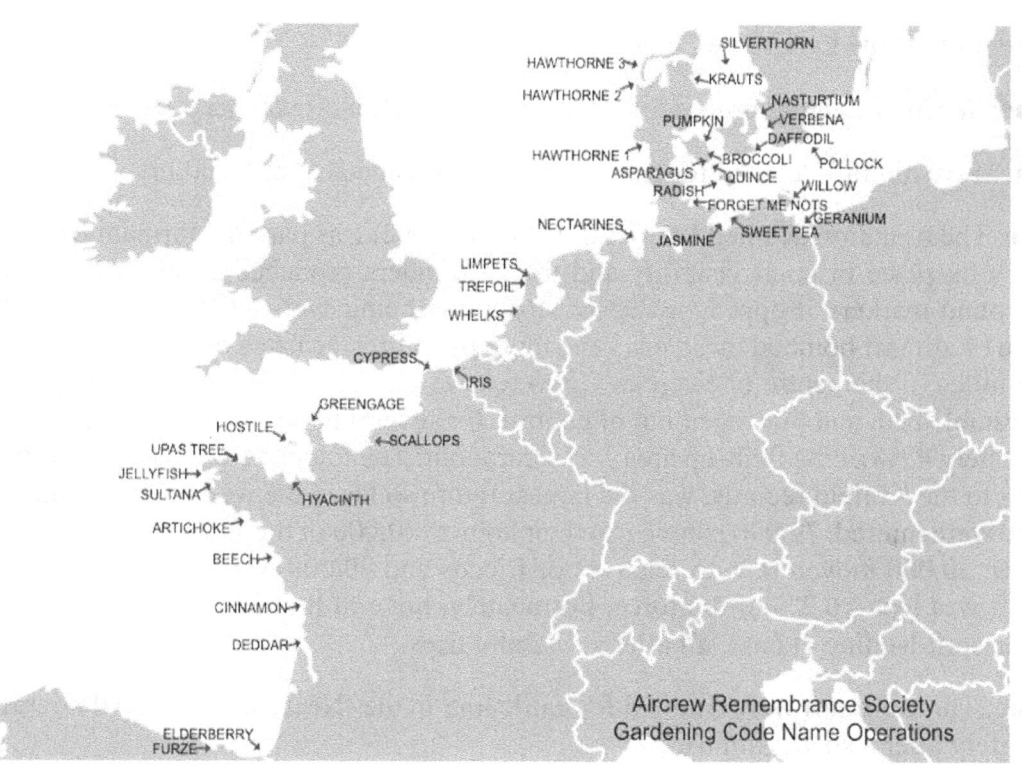

Gardening Code names and locations.

18th June: Film show to Aircrew, 'One Day of War'.

19th June: W/Cmdr Duguid proceeded on leave today, S/Ldr Alexander took over.

20th June: Five aircraft detailed for operations but was cancelled at 18.00 hrs.

21st June: The squadron detailed 14 aircraft to bomb Krefeld, as part of a formation of 705 aircraft. The raid took place in good visibility and the Pathfinders produced an almost perfect marking effort, ground-markers dropped by Oboe Mosquitos being well backed up by the Pathfinder heavies. 619 aircraft bombed these markers, more than three quarters of them achieving bombing within 3 miles of the centre of Krefeld. 2,306 tons of bombs were dropped. A large area of fire became established, and this raged out of control, for several hours. The whole centre of the city - approximately 47% of the built-up area - was burnt out. The total of 5,517 houses were destroyed, according to the Krefeld records, was the largest figure so far in the war. 1,056 people were killed and 4,550 were injured. 72,000 people lost their homes; 20,000 of these were billeted upon families in suburbs, 30,000 moved in with relatives or friends and 20,000 were evacuated to other towns. 44 aircraft was lost – 6.2% of the force. Fortunately, none of the losses was from 196 Squadron with all aircraft landing at base, all after successful trips.

22nd June: Three aircraft were detailed for gardening in the 'Nectarine' area. All aircraft returned to base safely after a successful trip.

On the same night twelve aircraft took off on a bombing raid on Mulheim, as part of a strength of 557 aircraft. The Pathfinders had to mark this target through a thin layer of stratus cloud, but reports indicate accurate initial marking. In later stages of the raid, the Pathfinder markers and the bombing moved slightly, into the northern part of the town, this had the effect of cutting all road and telephone communications with the neighbouring town of Oberhausen, with which Mülheim was linked for air-raid purposes. Not even cyclists or motorcyclists were able to get out of Mülheim, only messengers on foot could get through. The post-war British Bombing Survey Unit estimated that this single raid destroyed 64 per cent of the town of Mülheim. Heavy flak was encountered over the target area.

HE513 piloted by F/Sgt Watson was hit and holed in the port wing.

HE980 piloted by Sgt Gee sustained holes in the tail unit.

Both aircraft landed safely at base.

HE465 piloted by F/Sgt Hitchins was only shortly into the flight when his air speed indicator became u/s, so he returned to base with all the bomb load and landed safely.

23rd June: No flying activities. S/Ldr Alexander reported to the squadron as Wing Commander and assumed command from W/Cmdr Duguid who was posted away.

24th June: Sixteen aircraft joined a formation of 630 aircraft to bomb Wuppertal. This attack was aimed at the Elberfeld half of Wuppertal, the Barmen half of the town having been devastated at the end of May. The Pathfinder marking was accurate, and the main force bombing started well, but the creepback became more pronounced than usual. 30 aircraft bombed targets in more western parts of the Ruhr. Wuppertal was at the eastern end of the area. These bombing failures were probably a result of the recent run of intensive operations incurring casualties at a high level. However, much serious damage was again caused to this medium-sized Ruhr town. The post-war British survey estimated that 94 per cent of the Elberfeld part of Wuppertal was destroyed on this night. The aircrafts hit some heavy flak over the target area.

HE988 piloted by Sgt Griffiths sustained a hole in the tail section.

HE545 piloted by F/O Mallinson jettisoned his load not long after take-off due to a possibility of stalling, with the air speed indicator u/s and elevator control trouble.

LN432 piloted by P/O Sneddon, half a minute from the target, was hit by 8 incendiary bombs from another aircraft, and when returned to base was found to have the incendiaries lodged in the wings and fuselage. All aircraft were successful and returned to base safely.

25th June: The squadron detailed 5 aircraft on a gardening operation to the 'Artichoke's area. All aircraft were successful and returned to base safely.

On the same night eleven aircraft were part of a force of 473 aircraft sent to bomb Gelsenkirchen. The raid was not a success. The target was obscured by cloud and the Oboe Mosquito's, for once, failed to produce regular and accurate marking since 5 of the 12 Oboe aircraft found that their equipment was unserviceable. 30 aircraft was lost on the raid. One of them being from 196.

HE412 was shot down by a night fighter near Alphen aan de Rijn, Holland. Hit by the night fighter pilots Hauptmann Hans-Dieter Frank of the 2. /NJG 1 (flying a Bf 110 G-4 from Gilze-Rijen airfield) and Major Fritz Schaffer of the Stab/NJG 5. In the end, Hptm. Frank was credited with the victory. Four of the crew was killed but the bomb aimer Sgt E.H. Sandell survived the crash and was taken as a POW.

The crew was: Pilot: P/O Noel Bentley Smythe, Navigator: P/O George William Pollard, Wireless Operator: Sgt George Herbert William Peach, Air Gunner: Sgt Ronald Alfred Barlow, Bomb Aimer E.H. Sandell. The crew are buried in the Amersfoort (Oud Leusden) General Cemetery, Utrecht, Holland.

P/O Noel Bentley Smythe and crew. Noel was from Jamaica.

26th June: A general stand down today for aircrew.

27th June: Practice bombing and air to air firing carried out.

28th June: The squadron had sixteen aircraft join a force of 608 aircraft to bomb Cologne. The circumstances of this raid did not seem promising. The weather forecast said that Cologne would probably be cloud-covered although there might be a break. The Pathfinders had to prepare a dual plan. The target was cloud-covered and the less reliable sky marking system had to be employed. Only 7 of the 12 Oboe Mosquito's reached the target, and only 6 of these were able to drop their markers. The marking was 7 minutes late in starting and proceeded only intermittently. Despite all these setbacks, the main force delivered its most powerful blow of the Battle of the Ruhr. It was a good night for all and the squadron aircraft all had successful trips and returned to base with no incidents.

29th June: Four aircraft was detailed for gardening in the 'Artichoke' area. All aircraft dropped their mines and returned to base safely.

30th June: No flying due to adverse weather conditions

This concluded operations for June 1943.

The squadron had flown a total of 123 sorties in June, with the loss of just 3 aircraft, HE163, HE412 and MS486. The squadron also lost 6 aircrew.

July 1943

1st July: Instrument air tests were carried out.

2nd July: Four aircraft took off for a gardening operation in the Beeches area. All the aircraft was successful and landed away from base at Chivenor, Devon. On take-off from Chivenor to return to base, HE532 Piloted by Sgt Kogel crashed. The aircraft was badly damaged, but the crew escaped with no injuries.

3rd July: Fourteen aircraft joined a formation of 653 aircraft to bomb Cologne. The aiming point for this raid was the part of Cologne situated on the east bank of the Rhine. Much industry was located there. Pathfinder ground marking was accurately maintained by both the Mosquito Oboe aircraft and the backers-up, allowing the main force to carry out another heavy attack on Cologne. This night saw the first operations of a new German unit, Jagdgeschwader 300, equipped with single engined fighters using the Wilde Sau (Wild Boar) technique. In this, a German pilot used any form of illumination available over a city being bombed - searchlights, target indicators, the glow of fires on the ground - to pick out a bomber for attack. Liaison with the local flak defences was supposed to ensure that the flak was limited to a certain height above which the Wild Boar fighter was free to operate. The new German unit claimed 12 bombers shot down over Cologne but had to share the 12 available aircraft found to have crashed with the local flak, who also claimed 12 successes. Two of the aircraft lost that night were from 196.

HZ478 Piloted by F/O Eastwood and HE980 Piloted by Sgt Gee.

The crew: Pilot: F/O Eric Douglas Eastwood, Co-Pilot: F/O James Henry Stewart, Navigator: F/O Herbert Clifford Wheal, Bomb Aimer: F/Sgt Howard Langlands, Wireless Operator: Sgt Alfred Reginald Stone, Air Gunner: Sgt Morris Dixon, all are buried in the Gosselies Communal Cemetery, Charleloi, Belgium.

HZ478 was shot down by a German Night Fighter Piloted by Major W Herget based at Florennes Airbase south of Charleroi.

This was an exceptionally experienced crew. Together they had flown no fewer than 241 missions. Excluding F/O Stewart, who flew his first or second mission, they had an average of 48 missions. These men already had their first tour completed, thirty missions, then signed a second on a voluntary basis. Today they rest in Gosselies, they received no distinction for their efforts.

A Belgian researcher, Daniel Brasseur from Solre-sur-Sambre wrote:-

"Many inhabitants of Solre-sur-Sambre still remember the night of July 3-4th 1943 when a British bomber crashed near the village cemetery. They are all buried at the cemetery of Gosselies, near the city of Charleroi. It was on a hot summer night and some houses had their windows open when a deafening engine noise disturbed the tranquillity of the village. Some persons still remember the flames in the sky, the plane, the horrible explosion, the violent shock, the dispersed remains, the blazing fuel that flowed over the Emile Bosseau Street, and the dead who arrived to remind people this night that there was still a war going on. A blazing wing and an engine had crashed on the roof of the family Vigneron. M. Charlemagne Vigneron ensured his son was alive, and asked his wife and son to follow him to jump out of a window. Surprised in their sleep, Madame Vigneron and her son escaped the house by the back door. Everything was on fire and there were explosions all around. At that moment in Emile Bosseau Street, a wing from the plane crashed into the street. A ball of flame erupted, and Charlemagne Vigneron was trapped in his home where he suffered an appalling death. His wife and son were saved due to fleeing out of the back door. One engine crashed in the garden of M. Crigne, and the cockpit landed on the property of M Arnould, with the body of one of the RAF men still at his position. A second crewman's body was found nearby, and the other RAF men were found dead still wearing their parachutes ready to jump. A card showing the Wellington's flight plan was found in the garden of M. Delahaut in Pont Bara Street and he burned it due to fear of reprisals from the occupying Germans. Debris from the bomber was scattered over a wide area, and the Germans immediately barricaded the crash site and forbade all access. Strangers flocked to the village and rumours abounded that a crew member had survived, sadly not the case, and that a German officer, possibly Major Herget the pilot who shot the bomber down had gone to see his handy work. A recovery team, the Bergunskommando, arrived from the Gosselies airfield to remove the RAF men's bodies and the aircraft remains. It took two days to gather the wreckage of the bomber and load it onto trucks, so it could be taken by railroad to the recovery park in Paris where all the remains of allied planes which came down in Belgium were taken. The crew of the Wellington HZ478 was among millions of casualties of the Second World War, but these ones, the people of Solre-sur-Sambre would remember for generations".

HE980 was shot down at 0.55hrs near Averbode, Brabant, 6km NW Diest, Belgium, by Oblt. Heinz-Wolfgang Schnaufer.

The crew was: Pilot: F/Sgt Paul Gee, Navigator: Sgt Ronald Sydney Naile, Bomb Aimer: Sgt Allan Henry Taylor, Wireless Operator: Sgt George Neville Downing, Air Gunner: Sgt Albert James Horne. All are buried in the Heverlee War Cemetery, Vlaams-Brabant, Belgium

4th July: Six aircraft detailed for gardening but was cancelled at 18.00hrs.

5th July: Eight aircraft detailed for a gardening mission to the Lorient area. All laid their mines successfully and returned to base safely.

6th July: Eight aircraft again detailed to Lorient and again all successful apart from HF545 piloted by Sgt Holloway who had to turn back ninety minutes into the mission owing to the illness of the navigator.

7th July: The aircraft on previous night's gardening returned to base from Harwell. All operational crews stood down.

The crash site at Emile Bosseau Street. The geodetic fuselage of the Wellington can be seen in the foreground.

Two photos of navigator Howard Langlands taken pre-war, Left : Howard is on the far right standing, in the first photo at a summer camp in 1938, Right : second from right standing, playing for Hawthorn Leslies cricket team.

8th July: Two aircraft sent for gardening in the Trefoil area all returned to base safely.

9th July: No flying due to bad weather.

10th July: Crews again stood down due to weather.

HE980 and its crew who all perished on the night of 4th July 1943 and are all buried in the Haverlee War Cemetery, Belgium.

11th July: The squadron was stood down from operations. Some aircraft did some local flying and Wellington ZO-H piloted by F/O Mallinson made a successful belly landing after a tyre burst on take-off. All the crew was unhurt.

12th July: Eight aircraft was detailed for gardening in the Lorient area, all having successful trips, apart from HE178 piloted by Sgt Holloway, who had to turn back owing to the C.S.U. u/s, also the manual controls was sluggish and low revs on the starboard engine.

13th July: The squadron detailed nine aircraft to join a force of 374 aircraft - 214 Halifaxes, 76 Wellingtons, 55 Stirlings, 18 Lancasters and 11 Mosquitos ordered to bomb Aachen. A strong tail wind brought the first waves of the main force into the target area before zero hour with the result that, when the first Pathfinder markers were released, an unusually large number of aircraft bombed in the first minutes of the raid. The visibility was good and large areas of Aachen appeared to burst into flame at once. In the words of the report from Aachen, 'A *Terrorangriff* (terror attack) of the most severe scale was delivered. 20 aircraft - 15 Halifaxes, 2 Lancasters, 2 Wellingtons and 1 Stirling was lost, 5.3 per cent of the force. Of 196 Squadron all aircraft returned to base safely.

HE165 piloted by Sgt Kogel was hit by flak and holed in the port wing and fuselage.

HE685 piloted by F/Lt Ellis had both wings, the fuselage, port tail plane, front turret, and the bomb panel hit and holed by the predicted heavy flak.

HF545 piloted by F/Sgt Wakeley had to turn back early owing to part of the rear gunner's oxygen equipment being missing. His load of incendiaries was brought back. All aircraft landed safely.

14th July: Orders have been received for the squadron to move to Witchford, Ely, on the 19th July. All flying ceases as from today. The original intention was to move the squadron personnel and a large quantity of its equipment by glider, but circumstances prevent this and the move will be carried out by road and rail.

15th July: Thirteen crews left today for conversion units at Waterbeach, Stradishall and Woolfox Lodge.

16th July: An advance party of 32 under the command of S/Ldr Wigfall left Leconfield today for Witchford.

17th July: The squadron's heavy equipment was today loaded on to a train at Beverley. All personnel were engaged in packing.

18th July: Final preparation for the move was made today.

19th July: The squadron moved today by road and rail to R.A.F. Witchford. The move was accomplished without incident.

20th and 21st July: Settling in at Witchford.

22nd July: Two Stirling aircraft arrived today on allotment to the squadron.

23rd July: Aircrew personnel consisting of a few incomplete crew members went to 1651 C.U. at Waterbeach today.

24th July-31st July: There was nothing to report owing to the aircrew personnel being away at various conversion units, and some of the maintenance crews away at RAF Waterbeach.

This completed operations for 196 Squadron for July. The squadron had flown a total of 53 sorties in the month with the loss of two aircraft, HZ478 and HE980, with the loss of 11 aircrew. It also seems that another aircraft was lost to the squadron. HE171 was listed as lost in the Bomber Command losses but not in the squadron records. It was probably lost in a flying accident recorded in the squadron records but not with its identity number

From the very first sortie to cessation at this point all sorties were carried out on Vickers Wellington X Bombers.

In this time the Squadron undertook 609 Sorties with the loss of 21 Aircraft which represents a loss rate of 3.45%. They lost 82 Aircrew.

August 1943

1st August-10th August: There has been nothing to report owing to the aircrew personnel being away at various conversion units.

11th August-15th August: Aircrews are now returning from the conversion units.

16th August: Five sorties were flown today, (non-operational), three aircraft from 'A' flight and two from 'B' flight.

17th August: Air tests and cross country carried out. Aircrews continue to arrive.

18th August: Local flying and air to sea firing carried out.

19th August: One ferry collection trip to Stradishall and back.

20th August: Fighter affiliation carried out.

21st August: Local flying and fighter affiliation carried out.

22nd August: Same as yesterday.

23rd August: Cross country, load tests and local flying carried out.

24th August: The squadron made its first operational flights in the Stirling. Four aircraft took off on a sea search, but with no success, three aircraft returned but EH952 piloted by Sgt Brett failed to return.

The crew of EH952 was: Pilot: Sgt Percy William Brett, Navigator: Sgt Eric Walter John Kerr, Air Bomber: Sgt Douglas Henry Canning, W/Op: Sgt Louis Henry Huggins, F/Eng: Sgt Raymond Albert Treadwell, A/G: Sgt D.F. Moore, A/G: Sgt Edward Lawton.

Stirling EH952 ZO-A which was carrying a Lindholme Gear* and Stirling EF469 ZO-B would search the area 5456N-0425E-5456N-0530E-5564N-0530E-5504N-0425E while ZO-X and ZO-Z would search the area within 5504N-0425E-5504N-0530E-5512N-0530E-6512N-0425E. After having crossed the North Sea and having entered the search area, 'A' sighted some fishing smacks which the two Stirlings investigated. 'B' then saw another boat some distance away and went to investigate. While 'B' was away pilot Sgt P.W. Brett was forced to ditch EH952 approximately 65 nautical miles south west of Barren, (Barren is the location where a German Vorpostboot guarded the entrance to Esbjerg harbour), due to the loss of the two starboard engines at approximately 17:15 hrs. The tail struck first and broke away leaving a gaping hole where the tail plane had been. As the front end dipped into the sea, the crew clambered up to the opening, which was a two step forward, one step backwards exercise as the oil and the hydraulic fluid made it a difficult uphill climb. The whole crew got out and eventually entered the aircrafts dinghy which had been released automatically.

After having floated around for a period of time they spotted a fishing boat heading towards them. It was E 403 'Conni' of Esbjerg. Skipper Hans Kromack Christensen had seen the aircraft ditch and had set course for the dinghy. The crew was taken on board and given what dry clothes could be found and the dinghy was taken in tow. The fishing boat had been at sea for six days, but now wanted to return to the fishing ground to finish fishing, before they set course for Esbjerg. The Englishmen wanted the fishing boat to take them to Sweden, but due to lack of fuel that was not a possibility. On the next morning when E 403 'Conni' had set course for Esbjerg, a German Ju 88 flew over the fishing boat and when 'Conni' met with the most westerly German Vorpostboot by Skallingen, the Germans sent a guard of two marines on board the fishing boat and ordered it to sail direct to the traffic harbour. Here they arrived at 18:30 hours. Under German guard the airmen were taken to Küstenüberwachungsstelle and handed over to Kapitän Bösch. They were placed under guard in a nearby schoolhouse.

When interrogated by the Danish police, Skipper Christensen told them that he had sighted the aircraft ditch at 07:00 hours on the same morning, thus hiding that he had actually picked the crew up the day before but had continued fishing afterwards.

From Esbjerg, the aircrew were placed in a railway freight wagon and sent via Hamburg, to Dulag Luft at Oberursel near Frankfurt for interrogation. They arrived in Oberursel and stayed for a bit more than a week. They were then sent to Stalag IVB Mühlberg a.d.Elbe where they stayed until the end of war. They were released on 23/4/1945.

When Stirling 'B' returned to base at 18:24 hrs it reported that 'A' had last been sighted at 5458N 0525E which is approx. 97 nautical miles south west of Esbjerg.

*Lindholme Gear (Also known as Air Sea rescue Apparatus Mk 4) was a British air-dropped rescue equipment designed during the Second World War to aid survivors in the water. The Lindholme gear was developed at RAF Lindholme during the 1940s to provide a simpler rescue system than the air-dropped lifeboats then in use. The Lindholme Gear is a five cylinder-shaped container joined together by lengths of floating rope. The centre container would house a nine-man inflatable dinghy with the other containers housing survival such as emergency rations and clothing. The gear would be carried in the weapons bay of the aircraft and dropped in a long line, up-wind of the survivors. The dinghy would inflate on impact and then drift towards the survivors. The survivors can then use the dinghy and haul in the containers of equipment and await rescue.

25th August: Bomb load tests carried out.

Sgt. Percy William Brett *Sgt. Edward Lawton* *Sgt. Douglas Henry Canning*

26thAugust: Two aircraft where detailed for mine-laying, one did not take off owing to engine trouble, and the other piloted by F/O Mallinson had to abandon the mission when over the French coast owing to navigational equipment being faulty.

27th August: Three aircraft where detailed for mine-laying in the Frisian Islands, all dropped their mines and returned to base successfully.

28th August: Crews stood down owing to bad weather.

29th August: Six aircraft detailed for operations but was later cancelled.

30th August: Three aircraft was detailed for mine-laying in the 'Nectarine' area, all had successful trips.

Five aircraft where detailed to bomb Munchengladbach, all aircraft having successful trips, although they encountered bad weather, and returned to base safely.

31st August: Six aircraft where detailed to join a formation for the bombing of Berlin. Four aircraft completed the mission successfully.

EF492 piloted by Sgt Hitchings turned back just off Texel due to the mid-upper turrets intercom being u/s and unable to transmit, the pilot jettisoned the bombs in the sea on the return.

EH961 ZO-D piloted by Sgt Griffiths failed to return. EH961 was another victory for the ace Hauptman August Geiger. It crashed at 23.28hrs some 6 miles south of Enschede, Holland.

The crew was: Pilot: Sgt J. Griffiths, Navigator: Sgt C.P. Pierce, Bomb Aimer: F/O D.L.P. Justice, W/Op: Sgt I. Llewellyn, F/Eng: Sgt G.P. Poynter, A/G: Sgt G.S. Auld, A/G: Sgt G.A. Sperring. Three of the crew were killed, Sgt Pierce and F/O Justice and Sgt Llewellyn.

Funeral services for those who died were held on 2 September 1943 at the Enschede Easter General Cemetery. At 18, Sergeant Pierce RCAF was not only amongst the youngest Canadians killed on Bomber Command duties in 1943, but he was also one on the youngest navigators employed on operations. All the other members of the crew became Prisoners of War in the Stalag IVB, Muhlberg/Elbe camp for the duration of the war until the camp was liberated on 23/4/45 by the Russians.

This brought to an end the operations for the squadron in August.

The squadron flew a total of 18 sorties with the loss of 2 aircraft EH952 and EH961, with the loss of 3 aircrew.

Sgt John Griffiths.

F/Sgt Charles Phillip Pierce.

September 1943

1st September: Load test climbs carried out.

2nd September: Three aircraft were detailed for mine-laying in the 'Nectarine' area off the Frisian Islands. All aircraft returned to base safely, but EF494 piloted by F/Sgt Robbins, on inspection was found to have a hang up (bomb not dropped) owing to a failure of the electrical circuit.

3rd September: Four aircraft took off on a mine-laying operation to the Deodars area near Bordeaux. Three returned successfully, but EF114 piloted by F/Sgt Wakely was caught in search lights off Isigny. Fired at from 3000ft and returned fire, 500 rounds of ammo. The skipper thought it wise to return to base. Mines brought back.

4th September: Two aircraft detailed on a sea search with no results. Later the same night, four aircraft successfully completed a mine-laying operation to the Deodars.

5th September: Nine aircraft were part of a force to bomb Manheim. Most pilots reported having had a rough trip with many German night fighters about. Five aircraft were successful and landed back at base.

EF467 piloted by P/O Dyson had a combat with a fighter, which shot up one of the Stirling's engines, but got away and returned to base safely.

EE973 ZO-U piloted by S/Ldr Edmondson was hit by flak and his bomb aimer Sgt Redding received a splinter wound in the left eye. The damaged aircraft which had its undercarriage shot to bits and its outer starboard engine shot away, crash landed at base with no other injuries to crew. The aircraft being written off.

HE950 piloted by F/O Deans was badly shot up by a night fighter. Sergeant Butts was the rear gunner of the aircraft. Shortly after the bombs were released the aircraft was attacked by enemy fighters. In the first attack the bomber was hit, and Sergeant Butts' guns suddenly failed to operate. Nevertheless, this airman coolly gave his pilot directions in offensive action and at the same time cleared his guns of their stoppages. Further attacks were made by the enemy fighters but owing to Sergeant Butts' skilful commentary, Flying Officer Deans so manoeuvered his aircraft that one of the attackers was shot down. The Stirling landing safely at Newmarket.

For their actions on this night F/O Deans and F/Sgt Butts were awarded the DFC and DFM respectively. Gazetted on 5th October 1943 the citation was a joint one and reads:

'One night in September 1943, Flying Officer Deans and Sergeant Butts were pilot and rear gunner of an aircraft which attached Mannheim. Shortly after the bombs were released the aircraft was attacked by enemy fighters. In the first attack the bomber was hit and Sergeant Butts' guns suddenly failed to operate. Nevertheless, this airman coolly gave his pilot directions in offensive action and at the same time cleared his guns of their stoppages. Further attacks were made by the enemy fighters but owing to Sergeant Butts' skilful commentary, Flying Officer Deans so manoeuvered his aircraft that one of the attackers was shot down. This officer and airman displayed great skill and courage'.

Deans and three of his crew Butts, Vickers and Rothwell were leading a charmed life as they were the crew of Wellington HE163 which crashed on the 1st June.

EE964 ZO-F piloted by P/O Norris was lost over Bachenau, Heilbronn. Homeward bound, the aircraft was shot down by night fighter pilot Feldwebel Rudolf Frank of the 2. /NJG 3 based in Niedersachsen, the attack taking place at a height of 16,000ft. There were usually 7 crew on board, but on this aircraft, there was an extra pilot, presumably training. Seven of the crew perished and one was taken prisoner of war.

The crew was Pilot: P/O Frederick Norris, 2nd Pilot: P/O Richard Robert Whitaker, Navigator: F/Sgt Thomas Charles Foster, Flight Engineer: Sgt Glynville William Moss, Bomb Aimer: F/O Kenneth Arthur Charles Ayling, Wireless Operator: Sgt Francis Joseph Brown, Mid Upper Gunner: Sgt Avon Emrys Gomer Price, all the afore mentioned were all killed, rear gunner Sgt R. A. Newman was captured and was taken POW.

6th September: The squadron was stood down today.

7th September: Two load tests were carried out.

8th September: Eight aircraft took off as part of a bombing raid to Boulogne. Seven aircraft were successful, but EE874 Piloted by F/Sgt. Kogel returned early through engine trouble, jettisoned his load and extra fuel over the sea, and returned to base via Clacton.

9th September: Two air tests and some local flying were carried out.

10th September: No flying due to weather.

11th September: Same as yesterday

12th September: Load and air tests carried out by five aircraft.

13th and 14th September: No flying due to weather.

15th September: Twelve aircraft were detailed on a raid to Montlucon, but owing to a series of mishaps and mischances only nine took off. All aircraft returned to base successfully.

P/O Richard Robert Whitaker.

EF116 piloted by F/Sgt. Holloway had 8 incendiaries dropped on it from a Halifax above but had a lucky escape. One holed the fuselage above the bomb aimer, then falling between his legs, but he coolly removed the offending incendiary.

16th September: Eleven aircraft was detailed to bomb Modane. Ten were successful but EF114 ZO-H piloted by F/Sgt. Wakely was missing.

The crew of EF114 was: Pilot: F/Sgt Noel Nathaniel Wakely, Nav: F/O Harold Allen Nelson Kitchen, B/A: Sgt Alexander Sargant Taylor, W/Op: Sgt Stephen Thomas Flatman, F/Eng: Sgt Wilfred Albert Gilbert, A/G: Sgt Graham Francis Pyott, A/G: Sgt Gordon Esmond Kane.

EF114 was shot down by Feldwebel Herbert Penz of the 2./JG 2, flying an Fw 190A near Heurtevent, Calvados, Normandy. All the crew were buried in the Lisieux Communal Cemetery, France.

17th September: A housewarming party was held in the Officers Mess tonight and a good time was had by all.

18th September: Four aircraft were detailed on mining duties to the Cinnamon area. One failed to get away, two were successful but were diverted to Tangmere due to bad weather, and one turned back owing to encountering a severe electrical storm.

19th September: The two aircraft returned from Tangmere. Some air tests.

20th September: One aircraft went out on a sea search but returned with no success.

F/Sgt. Noel Nathaniel Wakely

The graves in the foreground of EF114s crew.

21st September: Two aircraft went on a minelaying operation to the 'Nectarine' area, both returned successful.

22nd September: Eleven aircraft were detailed to attack Hanover. Two did not take off, one owing to a shortage of personnel, it was not bombed up in time, and the other to an electrical fault. A third aircraft returned early due to the rear turret being u/s and runaway guns. All other aircraft returned safely after a successful sortie.

23rd September: Twelve aircraft were detailed to attack a target near Mannheim. One returned early through a fault, but the other eleven successfully bombed the target and landed back at base apart from one. EF492 landed at Tangmere due to an oil leak in one of the engines.

24th September: Two aircraft were detailed for minelaying in the 'Nectarine' area, both were successful, but when the second one, EH899 got back to base, the weather had considerably deteriorated and it took an hour to get them back down.

25th September: One aircraft was sent on minelaying to the 'Nectarine' area and returned successful.

27th September: Eleven aircraft set off to bomb Hanover. All had a successful trip.

EH932 had to land at Docking due to a lack of fuel.

BK663 ZO-K piloted by Sgt. Weaver, when over the target, was unable to release bombs owing to an electrical failure which caused malfunction of the bomb doors. Part of the load was jettisoned over target and part unknowingly brought back. The aircraft was hit in the tail by flak over the Dutch coast, and crashed into ground in bad visibility, one and half miles south east of Ely. The bomb aimer Sgt. Stern was seriously injured but the rest of the crew escaped with either slight or no injuries. The aircraft was written off.

28th September: No flying today

29th September: Two aircraft went out on a sea search but came back unsuccessful.

30th September: Some local flying carried out today.

This concluded operations for September. The squadron flew a total of 95 sorties. With the loss of 14 aircrew and 4 aircraft, EE973, EE964, EF114 and BK663.

October 1943

1ˢᵗ October: Eleven aircraft detailed for operations but was later cancelled.

2ⁿᵈ October: Seven aircraft were detailed on mining duties. Six to Kraut and one to 'Nectarine'. All were successful.

3ʳᵈ October: Eleven aircraft to bomb Kassel, but one failed to take off. The remainder found and bombed the target apart from EF464.

EF464 ZO-P, piloted by F/Sgt. Kogel, after reaching the Dutch coast, was attacked by a night fighter, and taking evasive action, caused the engines to over-rev and the port outer failed. F/Sgt Kogel turned back and made it across the North Sea for an emergency landing at Coltishall. The port inner then also failed and the Stirling hit trees and crashed at Scottow, a small village near the airfield. The flight engineer Sgt. Dickie was killed. The pilot Kogel was badly injured and the rest of the crew were either slightly injured or got away with nothing more than shock. Sgt Thomas Lynas Dickie was buried in the Knockbreda Cemetery, Belfast.

The crew was Pilot: G.H .Kogel, Nav: Sgt C.D. Williams, B/A: Sgt. A.W. Clarke, W/O: Sgt. R.L. George, F/Eng: Sgt T.L. Dickie, A/G Sgt J.A. Beattie, A/G: Sgt F. Reeves.

Short Stirling EF464 ZO-P

4th October: Six aircraft were detailed for a bombing raid on Frankfurt, but only five took off. All aircraft returned safely after a successful trip.

5th October: Local flying took place.

6th October: No flying due to bad weather.

7th October: Eight aircraft detailed for operations, five for a bombing mission and three for gardening. The weather was unsatisfactory so only the gardeners were ultimately dispatched to drop their vegetables in the 'Nectarine' area. All were successful with an uneventful trip.

8th October: Thirteen aircraft were detailed for operations, seven on a bombing raid and six minelaying. The bombing trip was to Bremen.

EF494 piloted by P/O Dyson, when over the North Sea, both starboard engines cut out and had to ditch in the sea at Hemsby, 5 miles north of Yarmouth. Apart from the bomb aimer F/Lft Luff, who suffered slight leg injuries, the rest of the crew were unscathed and managed to paddle to shore.

Sgt Thomas Lynas Dickie

EJ110 piloted by F/Sgt. Holloway had to return when the port inner engine became u/s. He jettisoned the bombs and returned to base. EF468 piloted by F/O Deans returned early owing to the starboard engine throttle sticking. He too jettisoned his bombs and returned to base. All the other aircraft successfully bombed Bremen.

Of the six due to lay mines only four took off, laying their mines in the Cinnamon area, but landed at Mepal due to fog at base.

9th October: The four aircraft returned from Mepal.

10th October: One aircraft carried out a sea search but returned with no sightings.

11th and 12th October: No flying due to bad weather.

The remains of EF494 at Hemsby Gap, Norfolk.

13th October: Air tests and formation flying.

14th October: Air tests and local flying.

15th October: Air tests and local flying.

16th October: Air tests, practice bombing and cross country.

17th October: Four aircraft took-off on minelaying duties. Two to Cinnamon and two to 'Nectarine's. Three were successful but EE972 returned early due to Gee being u/s shortly after take-off. On the way back, they ran into an electrical storm, but returned to base safely.

On the same morning, EH960 ZO-X piloted by F/O Deans took off on an air test and nothing more was heard.

EF960 had been test flown two days earlier and a pronounced shuddering in flight reported. F/O Deans made a few adjustments, and the Station Engineer Officer ordered another test. The aircraft was airborne at 1050 hrs and was not seen again. EH960 crashed into the Wash twelve miles off Kings Lynn.

The crew was Pilot: F/O James Lyall Deans DFC, Nav: F/O Frederick John Chapman, F/Eng: Sgt Kenneth Leonard Wallace, W/O: Sgt James Lionel Lane A/G: Sgt Terence McDonnell, A/G: F/Sgt Nolan Butts DFM, and the Squadron Engineer Officer F/Ltn John Gordon Griffiths. F/O Chapman was buried at Cambridge City Cemetery, W/O Lane was buried at Abney Park Cemetery and Sgt Wallace was buried at Great Bircham Cemetery, all the rest are remembered on the Runnymede Memorial

Flying Officer James Lyall Deans DFC

At the time off the crash F/O Deans had 102 hours 30 minutes on Stirlings.

F/O Deans and F/Sgt Butts luck had finally run out.

F/O Deans and F/Sgt Butts were in the crew of HE163 in June when the Wellington they were flying in crashed at Arram Grange. The same crew were in HE950 in September when they were attacked by a night fighter. It was for their actions in HE950 that F/O Deans was awarded the DFC, and F/Sgt Butts was awarded the DFM.

18th October: Local flying carried out.

F/Sgt Nolan Butts DFM

Deans with other aircrew of 196 Squadron.

19th October: Fighter affiliation carried out.

20th October: One aircraft on a gardening sortie to 'Nectarine's which was successful.

21st October: Air tests.

22nd October: Air to sea firing.

23rd October: No flying today.

24th October: Two aircraft carried out a sea search but nothing sited.

On the same day four aircraft were detailed for mining. Two were scrubbed before take-off, and one had engine trouble and did not take off. The other completed its sortie successfully to 'Nectarine'.

25th October: No flying.

26th October: One aircraft was detailed for mining in 'Nectarine's, which was successful, but was diverted to Lossiemouth on return due to bad weather at base.

27th, 28th and 29th October: No flying due to bad weather.

30th October: Three aircraft detailed for operations but was later cancelled.

31st October: No flying.

The month of October saw the Squadron fly a total of 54 Sorties with the loss of 8 aircrew and 3 aircraft. EF464, EF494 and EH960.

November 1943

1st November: No flying

2nd November: Some local flying.

3rd November: One aircraft was detailed for mining in the 'Nectarine's, all mines laid in allotted position. Aircraft returning to base successful.

4th November: Air to air firing and fighter affiliation.

5th November: Cross country flights.

6th November: No flying.

7th November: Air to air firing and cross country.

8th November: No flying.

9th November: The squadron celebrated the anniversary of its birthday and in the honour of the occasion there was a large party held in the officer's mess.

10th November: Two aircraft went on a sea search but there were no sightings. In the evening, three aircraft were detailed on a mining operation to Deddars. One failed to take-off, but the other two were successful, and on their return landed at Tangmere.

11th November: Load tests and circuits and landings.

12th November: Word was received today from RAF Sutton Bridge that the body of Sgt. J.L. Lane had been washed ashore from the Wash. Sgt, Lane was one of the crew lost on the 17th October when EH960 disappeared and was not heard of again.

13th November: News was received today that the squadron was to leave Witchford on the 18th and that 115 Squadron equipped with Lancasters are to come here instead. The squadron is to go Leicester East, taking with it all aircraft and ground equipment.

14th November: Nothing to report.

15th November: Air tests.

16th November: Circuits and bumps.

17th November: Preparation to move squadron.

18th November: The squadron moved from Witchford to Leicester East. As well as the transfer of the squadron to the new station, it was also transferred from No.3 Group Bomber Command to 38 Group, Allied Expeditionary Air Force (AEAF).

196 Squadron had flown its last operational mission with Bomber Command on the night of the 10/11 November 1943.

Twenty aircraft flew over between 10.40 and 1600 hours. The main party travelled by rail and arrived the same day.

19th to the 24th November: There was no flying, the squadron was occupied in settling into their new accommodation.

25th November: The squadron carried out some local flying.

26th November: Some local flying with one aircraft landing at Wymeswold.

27th to 30th November: No flying due to bad weather.

November saw only 5 Operations flown with no loss of aircrew or aircraft.

December 1943

1st to the 3rd December: There was no activities.

4th December: Wing Commander N. Alexander went to Honeybourne, taking as passenger, Group Captain R.E. Wintras O.C. RAF Leicester East.

5th and 6th December: No activities.

7th December: As in the past week, little flying has been possible owing to the extremely bad weather. Every opportunity has been taken to carry on with ground training and lectures to the aircrews and have been given by officers from a glider towing squadron of 38 Group, who have been attached to this unit for the purpose.

8th to 10th December: No activities due to bad weather.

11th December: W.C. Alexander proceeded to Broadwell for a conference, to ascertain whether this station would be suitable for training purposes.

12th December: No activities again.

13th December: Cross country flights were arranged for today, almost immediately after take-off visibility closed in.

14th to 17th December: No flying due to bad weather.

18th December: Cross country arranged, but again the weather closed in and the aircraft was diverted to Gamston.

19th December: No flying.

20th December: Group Captain Alvey from 38 Group Headquarters visited the squadron and explained the position regard to establishments and manning, and the different procedure in the matter of postings etc., now that the squadron is in the A.E.A.F. and not in Bomber Command.

21st December: Three aircraft were on night cross countries, and all three were diverted to Hixon, owing to an aircraft being bogged at base and obstructing the runway.

22nd December: The three aircraft returned from Hixon.

23rd December: The Air Officer Commanding of 38 Group, today gave a talk to all personnel on the subject of the future roll of the squadron.

24th December: No flying.

25th December: Christmas Day, the squadron stood down today. Many personnel took advantage of the numerous offers of hospitality made by the people of Leicester and the neighbourhood, and a good time was had by all.

26th to the 30th December: No activities due to bad weather.

The squadron flew no sorties in the month of December.

January 1944

1st January: A preliminary warning signal was received today that the squadron is to move to RAF Tarrant Rushton on the 7th.

2nd January: The Movement Control Officers for road and rail came from Nottingham today to discuss the impending move with the Commanding Officer.

3rd January: No activity.

4th January: An advance party consisting of 2 officers and 39 other ranks left this morning for Tarrant Rushton.

5th January: A start was made today on the loading of the equipment train, and by nightfall all the 40 trucks had been ready for dispatch tomorrow.

6th January: Kits and bicycles were loaded on to the personnel train today. The equipment train left for Wimborne tonight at 22.00 hours.

7th January: The squadron moved from Leicester East to Tarrant Rushton by air, rail and road. Four aircraft were unable to take off for various reasons. The main rail party arrived without incident, but the road party is not due until tomorrow, as they cannot get further than Yattendon in the day.

8th January: The road convoy arrived today.

9th January: No activity.

10th January: Two aircraft arrived from Leicester East.

11th and 12th January: No flying due to bad weather.

13th January: Nothing to report.

14th January: Four cross country flights were done and some local flying.

15th January: No flying due to fog.

16th January: Five glider towing sorties took place and there was also two cross country flights.

17th January: No flying today.

18th January: Nothing to report.

19th January: No flying today.

20th January: The weather had improved considerably, and some flying was possible. Some circuit and bumps.

21st January: A considerable amount of glider towing was indulged in today, and there was also some night flying.

22nd January: No flying.

23rd January: There were a range of different flying practice.

24th January: Nothing to report.

25th January: Glider towing.

26th January: No flying

27th January: More glider towing was undertaken.

28th January: A range of different flying, glider towing, cross country and formation flying.

29th January: There was the first mass take-off with Horsas and was very successful, all six getting off in 5 minutes 25 seconds. There was also some night towing for the first time.

30th January: There was again various flying duties.

31st January: No flying due to bad weather.

The squadron flew no sorties in January.

February 1944

1st February: No flying.

2nd February: Local flying.

3rd February: Two aircraft were detailed for an S.O.E. operation.

BK771 piloted by S/Ldr Edmondson swung on take-off and colliding with a Halifax of 298 Squadron which was stationary. The aircraft was partially burned but the crew and five passengers for Hurn escaped with their lives.

The other piloted by P/O F.T. Powell successfully carried out his mission. Another aircraft was sent out in place of the crashed one but could not locate its objective.

4th February: Four aircraft set off from Hurn on a special mission. Three returned safely after reaching the drop zone but EJ110 failed to return.

Monument to the crew of Stirling EJ110

EJ110 ZO-N piloted by P/O/ H.I. Pryke was completing a supply mission to the French Resistance. While overflying Ain in snow falls, the aircraft went out of control and crashed in Bois de Valorse, near Hauteville-Lompnes.

EJ110s crew was Pilot: P/O. Henry Ivan Pryke, F/Eng: Sgt. Robert Dowzer, A/B: W/O. James Donaldson, W/O: Sgt. Kenneth Albert Glew, Nav: Sgt. Alfred Spray, A/B: Sgt. Kenneth Thomas Staple, A/G: Sgt. Dennis Tunnard Vince. All the crew are buried in the Lyon French National Cemetery.

5th February: Three aircraft were detailed for operations to France. Two were successful.

EF469 ZO-B piloted by F/O Moore on a parachute drop to the resistance for the S.O.E., for the benefit of the Vosges resistance, crashed.

The crew was: Pilot: F/O. Thomas Moore, Nav: P/O. John Rothwell Lindley, A/B: W/O. Lionel Howard Woodruff, W/OP: Sgt. A.J. Cardiff, F/Eng: Sgt. Gordon Hemmings, A/G: F/Sgt. B.H. Town. A/G: Sgt. J.F. Bartlet.

F/O. Moore, P/O. Lindley and W/O. Woodruff were killed and were buried in Cornimont Cemetery. The remaining crew all became POWs.

Gordon Hemmings would later recall:

"The Stirling was taken into a hangar and loaded up with the containers for an S.O.E. operation that night. The aircrafts all up weight was 73,500lbs. This was well over the limit and we complained about it, but we were told it was necessary. We took-off and the aircraft only just cleared the perimeter at Hurn by a few feet.

We were in France and flying along a valley following a river with mountains well above the height of the aircraft. We came round a bend and ran into a curtain of snow. The pilot pulled up and opened the throttles but the aircraft hit a mountain at Le Menil Thillot-Cornimont and caught fire. The pilot, navigator and bomb aimer were all killed but the two gunners were uninjured and were soon captured, myself and the wireless operator, an Irishman, managed to get out and we met up later. We took shelter in a wooden hut but later had to ask the French to hand us over to the Germans due to burns etc."

6th February: Three aircraft were detailed for operations but were later cancelled.

7th February: No flying.

8th February: Three aircraft set off for Hurn on a special mission, of these, two reached their objective, but the third, although he reached it, did not receive the co-operation he looked for. All returned safely to Hurn.

9th and 10th February: Aircraft were detailed for operations but did not take-off due to bad weather.

11th February: One aircraft operated from Hurn and returned to base after an unsuccessful trip.

F/Lt. M.E.H. Dawson and F/O. T.B. Gittings were both awarded the Distinguished Flying Cross.

12th February: The Commander in Chief visited the station today and gave a talk to all aircrew personnel. Preparations were made for an exercise tomorrow, the intention of which is to land a glider borne brigade group of the 6th Airborne Division on Aldermaston Airfield. Ten aircraft of this squadron are to participate.

13th February: The exercise planned the night before was cancelled due to bad weather.

14th February: Local flying.

15th February: Local flying.

16th and 17th February: No flying

18th February: Nine aircraft took part in a glider towing exercise.

20th February: EF468 piloted by W/O. C.H. Hunter took off on a cross country operation but crashed at Bussey Stool Farm, Tarrant Gunville, six miles due north of Tarrant Rushton. The cause of the crash was unknown. All the crew were killed, and the aircraft was burnt out.

W/O Lionel Howard Woodruff.

The monument in the mountains where EF469 crashed.

The monument in Cornimont Cemetery for the crew of EF469.

The Rupt de la Sauce chalet then and now where Gordon Hemmings and Alan Cardiff found refuge.

Short Stirling Mk.IV EF469 ZO-B.

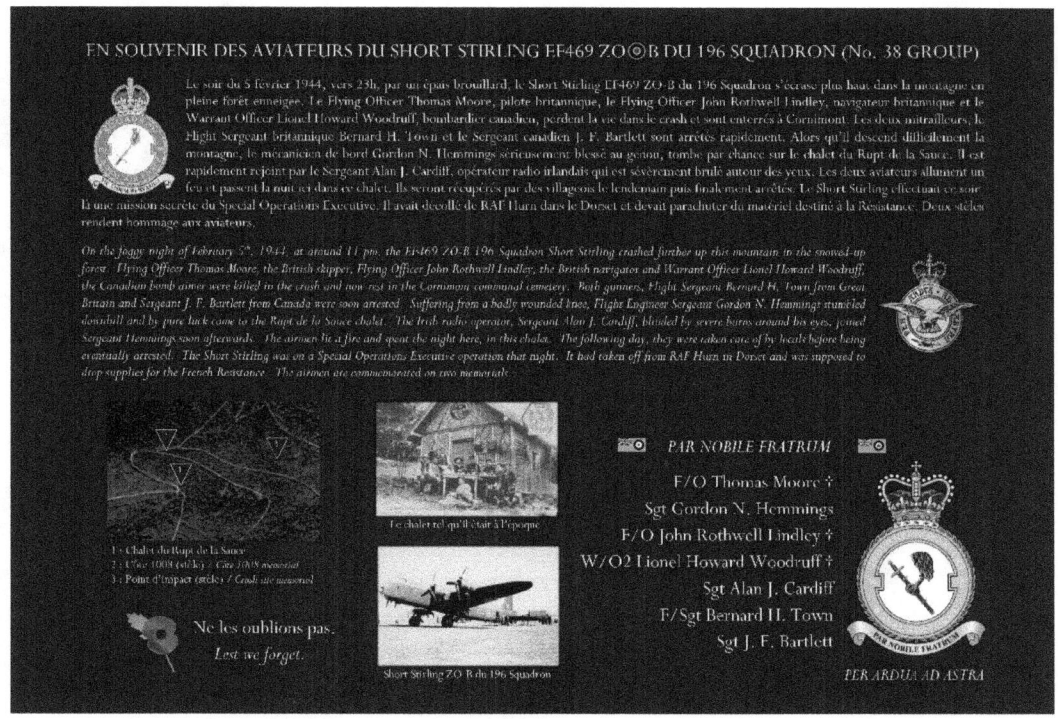

The plaque that is on display next to the chalet.

The crew of EF468 was: Pilot: W/O. Calvert Hamilton Hunter, Nav: F/Sgt. Ronald Cecil Lysons, W/O: Sgt. Duncan Malcolm McCannell, F/Eng: Sgt. John Edward Sawford, A/B: W/O. Charles Arthur Simpson, A/B: F/Sgt. Patrick William Sullivan.

The wireless op. Duncan McCannell's brother Munro was also killed on 6th June flying a Dakota of 233 Sqn.

21st to 28th February: Local flying and exercises were carried out.

29th February: Two aircraft were detailed for operations, but they were cancelled.

EF297 while landing at Netheravon to retrieve a Horsa, burst a port tyre causing it to swing and the undercarriage collapsed. The aircraft was eventually repaired and transferred to the parachute training school (P.T.S.) in May.

The month of February saw the squadron fly 13 sorties with the loss of 16 aircrew, 3 POWs and 4 aircraft, BK771, EJ110, EF468 and EF469.

March 1944

1st March: Some container dropping practice carried out in conjunction with cross country. Two sorties on air to ground firing practice.

2nd March: 119 Ratings of the Fleet Air Arm attached to the squadron arrived today. All are tradesmen intended to fill the deficiencies which exist following the bringing in of a new establishment for the squadron, and for the new servicing echelon.

3rd March: Two aircraft were detailed for operations, the take-off as usual from Hurn. One aircraft turned back from the French coast with engine trouble, and the other found it's D.Z. but was unable to complete its mission as there was snow on the ground.

It has now been settled that the move of the main party to Keevil will take place on the 14th. The advance party consisting of two officers and 44 ordinary ranks left today by glider and duly arrived.

4th March: Three aircraft were detailed for operations from Hurn, but later after the aircraft had got there, two of them were cancelled. The third, EF273 piloted by F/Sgt. Green, took off and returned to Hurn but the mission was not successful.

5th March: Three aircraft detailed for operations went to Hurn but were cancelled.

6th March: Five aircraft were detailed for operations. All took off and found the dropping zones but only one found the co-operation which enabled him to complete his mission successfully.

7th March: Five aircraft were detailed for operations but were later cancelled.

8th and 9th March: Many aircraft were engaged in practice exercises.

10th March: No flying due to bad weather.

11th March: Five aircraft were detailed for operations to France, but only four took off. All of them found their allotted targets but found no co-operation on the ground so had to bring their loads home.

12th March: No flying today in view of the impending move of the squadron to RAF Keevil. The day was spent by all sections in packing up.

13th March: Packing and loading gliders all day.

14th March: The road party got away, but the weather was none too good for flying, and only 10 gliders managed to get to Keevil before it clamped down altogether. These 10 gliders carried for the most part equipment, and very few personnel.

15th March: The move continued all day. Tug pilots towing loaded Horsas and returning to Tarrant Rushton with empty Horsas. Aircrew and ground crew did remarkably well on loading and ferrying.

16th March: Continued to move by air. One Horsa became detached and crashed through a Nissen hut but the crew were uninjured. Stirling LJ834 piloted by F/Sgt Lyons overshot the runway at Tarrant Rushton in rain using clear vision panel. It swung to avoid the boundary and the undercarriage collapsed. The aircraft was eventually repaired and transferred to the parachute training school (P.T.S.) in May.

17th March: Only four Horsa loads left to move and five tugs. All aircraft took off and landed safely at Keevil by 1300hrs.

18th and 19th March: There was no flying while the squadron settled in to the new station.

20th March: Thirteen aircraft were detailed for Group Exercise 'Bizz I', only eleven took off due to two developing magneto drops just prior to take-off.

21st March: Four aircraft ferried from Keevil to Tilstock, old Mark III Stirlings. Two aircraft did local towing, and three aircraft took-off to retrieve gliders from Brize Norton.

22nd March: Ten aircraft and crew were detailed to retrieve Horsas from Brize Norton. Five took-off and retrieved Horsas, remainder stopped before take-off as Brize Norton were not ready.

23rd March: Aircraft detailed to retrieve party from Tarrant Rushton.

24th March: One aircraft from Tarrant Rushton to Tilstock. Two aircraft on cross country. Six aircraft to Marham on Horsa retrieval. Four aircraft on local towing.

25th March: Ten aircraft and crews took part in a group exercise 'Bizz II'. One Horsa cast off when caught in the slipstream. The exercise was most successful.

26th March: Four aircraft on cross country in the morning. Six aircraft on retrieval of Horsas from Brize Norton. Five abortive sorties due to Brize Norton not being ready.

27th March: Three aircraft to Brize Norton to retrieve Horsas. One aircraft to Tarrant Rushton with S/Ldr. Brown to collect one Oxford aircraft for training. One aircraft to Ashbourne carrying F/Lt. Carmon DFC on posting. 'D' piloted by P/O. Pryse swung off runway on landing and undercarriage collapsed.

28th March: One aircraft with three crews to retrieve two aircraft which went u/s at Brize Norton. One aircraft with two crews to Tarrant Rushton, one crew to ferry one aircraft to Tilstock which was left at Tarrant Rushton. Crew returned from Tilstock by train. LJ839 piloted by F/Sgt. Green, when landing into the sun at Marham overshot and crashed through a blister hangar. All the aircrew were unhurt. LJ839 was written off.

29ᵗʰ March: No flying.

30ᵗʰ March: One aircraft detailed for operation to France. LJ845 piloted by F/Sgt. Oliver was reported missing, but later was found to have landed away.

31ˢᵗ March: One aircraft detailed for operation to France which was successful. Other exercises undertaken. F/Sgt. Oliver arrived back at base.

The month of March saw the squadron fly 13 sorties with no loss of aircrew and with the loss of 2 aircraft, LJ834 and LJ839.

April 1944

With the move to RAF Keevil the base is now shared with 299 Squadron.

1st April: No flying due to bad weather conditions.

2nd April: No flying in the morning due to bad visibility. The squadron took advantage off 299 Squadron not towing in their allotted time, and starting towing at 1500hrs and completed 21 lifts by dusk.

3rd April: No flying due to weather.

4th April: Fourteen aircraft and crews were briefed for exercise 'Drone', at 1330hrs. Aircrafts were marshalled by 1600hrs. First took-off at 1809hrs. Take off went quite well, tugs came onto the runway from the left, Horsas from the right. Time allowed for between take-off was two minutes, which was maintained. The weather on the forming up route was good, on the run up to the group R.V. low cloud was encountered. This cloud base was 700ft. and the hills were 900ft. Combinations tried to stay beneath base but were forced to climb through it. During this period 4 gliders cast off.

LJ842 ZO-K piloted by F/Sgt. Lees and glider crashed with complete loss of life in both machines. The aircraft, with the cloud at 700ft and hills at 900ft, hit a tree and crashed later one mile SW of Romsey, Hants. A report into the accident stated:

'The Horsa had either just cast off, or the rope broke near Petersfield, and the tug was probably heading for base. The reasons for the crash are unclear. LJ842 was seen flying over Romsey at a low altitude and not in any apparent difficulty. It was possible that the pilot was flying above 10/10ths cloud over Winchester and came down to see where he was, but got too low, and in avoiding a slight hill over Romsey, the aircraft stalled, and it struck the ground at a fairly steep angle'.

The crew was: Pilot: WO John Hugh Lees, F/Eng: Sgt Shayrene Meera, Nav: F/O John Robert Teece, A/B: Sgt John Thomas Wilkinson, W/Op: Flt Sgt Kenrick Payne, A/G: Sgt Sidney Claypole.

Sergeant John Hugh Lees, 1st Left Back Row.

WO Lees and Flt Sgt Payne are buried in the Bath Cemetery, Somerset. Sgt Meera is buried in the Gateshead East Cemetery. FO Teece is buried in the Dudley Churchyard. Sgt Wilkinson is buried in the South Shields Cemetery. Sgt Claypole is buried in the Nottingham Church Cemetery.

The remainder broke cloud and carried on at 200ft until approaching target R.V. when a descent was made to 1450ft. under cloud. A good concentration was obtained over the L.Z. and gliders cast off on time. Conditions on return to base were favourable for the first aircraft, but rain developed in later stages of the landing period.

5th April: Six aircraft carried out retrieval from the L.Z. of Horsas dropped on the fourth.

Three aircraft were detailed for operations to France, two successful, one not.

6th April: The squadron carried out its first paratrooper dropping, three aircraft taking part. Exercise was quite successful, but some snags were encountered which will have to be smoothed out. Modification for jumping still rather in the experimental stage.

7th April: No flying due to weather.

8th April: One aircraft to Tarrant Rushton with another crew to collect a/c 'V' which was left there but burst a tyre on landing so both crews returned in a/c 'V'.

9th and 10th April: Local flying and exercises were carried out.

11th April: Two aircraft detailed for operation to France, but only one took off due to the other aircraft being u/s. P/O Powell reached his objective, but due to heavy ground defences was unsuccessful. Other aircraft took part in exercises.

12th April: Local towing was carried out and others did troop dropping.

13th April: The station did a mass take-off with 24 combinations, to give air troops experience. The average take-off for 196 Squadron was one- and three-quarter minutes, the aircraft and Horsas coming in from the perimeter and connecting up. Three details of container dropping and four details of paratroop dropping were carried out.

14th April: F/O. Turner DFM, a new member of the squadron, did some circuits and landings, then local towing. F/O Turner has done some 90 operations as a gunner prior to joining the squadron as a pilot.

15th April: Local flying was carried out with Horsas.

16th April: Some flying was done but cut short early due to bad weather.

17th April: Twenty lifts were carried out. During this period F/Sgt King, a new pilot, had the misfortune to have his undercarriage stick. He came in to do a crash landing and did it very satisfactorily with a minimum amount of damage to the aircraft.

18th April: More various training flights, towing, container dropping and paratroop dropping carried out.

19th to 27th April: Every day was used as practice in paratroop dropping, glider towing, container dropping, practice mass take-offs and cross country amongst other various flying.

28th April: Three aircraft were detailed for operations to France. F/Sgt. James and F/Sgt. Fordham were successful, but F/Sgt King was unsuccessful.

29th April: Three aircraft were detailed for operations to France. W/O. Azouz was successful, but F/Sgt. Campbell and F/Sgt. Green were unsuccessful, and LJ837 flown by F/Sgt. Green received flak damage but returned to base safely.

30th April: Two crews were detailed to France. W/Cmdr. Alexander's aircraft was u/s so cancelled, while F/O. Arnold completed the mission.

Mass take-offs were again part off a series of exercises.

The month of April saw the squadron carry out 10 sorties with the loss of 6 aircrew and 1 aircraft, LJ842.

May 1944

1st and 2nd May: The squadron undertook local flying, glider towing and cross-country flights.

3rd May: Four crews were detailed for S.O.E. operations to France. All aircraft leaving from Tarrant Rushton. The aircrafts being piloted by F/Lt. Vanrenen, F/Sgt. Tait, F/Sgt. Hancock and F/Sgt. Waltrich. All were long trips but successful and returned to base safely.

EF309 piloted by F/Sgt. Waltrich sustained some flak damage.

4th May: Five crews on local towing.

5th May: Two crews were detailed for an S.O.E. operation to France, again from Tarrant Rushton. Both aircraft encountered light flak on route. W/O. Tickner had a successful trip but F/Sgt. Breed was unsuccessful due to no reception at drop zone.

6th May: Two crews were detailed on an S.O.E operation to France, again from Tarrant Rushton. The aircrafts being piloted by S/Ldr. Angell and F/Sgt Sargant, both ops failed due to no reception at drop zone.

7th May: Five aircraft were detailed for S.O.E. operations to France from Tarrant Rushton. W/Cmdr. Alexander was unsuccessful due to no reception at drop zone. F/O. Light, F/Sgt Campbell, F/O. Baker and F/Sgt King were all successful. On the way back F/Sgt. King saw a train below with a flak wagon on it. He therefore attacked and shot it up.

Back at base, training flights continued.

Pilot F/Sg R.W. Sargant and his crew. Nav: Sgt C .Westoby, A/B: W/O Bakogeorge, W/Op: F/Sgt E.R. Donald, F/Eng: F/Sgt P.C. Adcock, A/G: F/Sgt S.V. Carne.

F/Sgt R.W. Sargant of crew in front of LJ928 ZO-L

Sgt Peter Charles Alcock, flight engineer in Sargant's crew.

Short Stirling Mk.IV LK403 ZO-W.

8th May: Two crews were detailed for an S.O.E. operation to France, again from Tarrant Rushton. F/O. Arnold and F/Lt. Askew dropped 20 Containers and 2 Panniers successfully. Although there was flak guns on each side, they were so inaccurate, they did not trouble the aircraft.

9th May: Exercise 'Drongo', fifteen crews took part and successfully dropped paratroopers by night.

10th May: Five crews were detailed on S.O.E. operations to France from Tarrant Rushton. S/Ldr Brown and W/O. Tait were successful, but F/Sgt Green, F/Sgt. Fordham and W/O. Oliver were unsuccessful due to no reception.

W/O. Oliver's rear gunner baled out over enemy territory. Reasons unknown.

11th to 27th May: The squadron carried out exercises. Mass take-offs with gliders, cross country, formation flying and radar training.

28th May: Two crews on S.O.E. operations to France from Tarrant Rushton. F/Sgt Hoystead and F/Sgt. Prowd were both successful.

30th May: Two aircraft on S.O.E. operations to France from Tarrant Rushton. F/Sgt. Hill and W/O. Oliver were both unsuccessful.

This concluded flying for the month of May.

The month of May saw the squadron carry out 24 sorties with the loss of no aircraft. One aircrew Sgt. F.R. Rowe the rear gunner was posted as "Missing".

June 1944

Since the squadrons transfer to No. 38 groups it had carried out many 'cloak and dagger' operations which included supply dropping to resistance forces and the dropping of S.A.S. and S.O.E. parachutists over occupied territories. Operating alone, and at very low level each full moon period, was the time for S.O.E. and S.A.S. operations. These were highly secret at 200ft or 300ft almost always in moonlight over the D.Z. Since its move to Keevil, the constant training, especially with the Horsa Glider, was obvious to the crews something huge was on the horizon. This was it the 'Big One'. The squadron had learned just hours before they were about to take to the skies, that the invasion of Europe was about to start. Operation Overlord was about to start.

1st June: One crew on radar training and two crews on local towing.

2nd June: Two crews on radar cross country.

3rd June: Two crews on local towing.

4th June: Four crews went to Upavon to ferry back spare aircraft.

5th June: Twenty three aircraft were detailed on Operation Tonga, to drop paratroopers of the British 6th Airborne Division in Normandy, France at "D.Z. N". Each aircraft carried 20 troops plus kit bags, containers and cycles. First up was W/Com. Alexander at 23.20 hrs. All aircraft and gliders being airborne within 50 minutes. All aircraft encountered concentrated flak over D.Z.

Of the 23 aircraft, 13 were successful with no mishaps.

LJ810 piloted by S/Ldr. Angell dropped the troops and containers, but the cycle got caught up in the strops and was not dropped. Otherwise, successful.

EF234 piloted by F/O. Powell dropped all troops and containers but the 19th paratrooper hesitated, so the aircraft had to make a second run over the D.Z. which resulted in several hits from flak in the fuselage and port wing.

LK510 piloted by F/Lt Vanrenen dropped all troops and containers successfully but was badly hit by flak over the D.Z. but managed to land o.k. at base.

LJ836 piloted by F/Lt Askew completed his drop but one paratrooper was hit by the S/O engine.

LJ 502 piloted by W/O. Holloway was successful but was hit in the port wing.

LJ845 piloted by F/Sgt Hancock had trouble getting strops in after dropping but were successful.

LJ440 piloted by F/O. Baker dropped successfully over D.Z. but was very badly hit by flak, which put two engines u/s. When over the sea, pilot Baker gave the order to prepare to bale out, unfortunately the navigator and bomb aimer only heard part of the message and baled out.

The crew of LJ440 was: Pilot: F/O Baker, Nav: F/O Anderson, A/B: F/Ltn Luff DFC, W/Op: W/O Pearce, F/Eng: Sgt Bond, A/G: F/Sgt McGovern.

Richard Luff DFC, the squadron bomb aimer was never found, and his name is remembered along with all other aircrew with no known grave on the RAF Runnymede Memorial overlooking the River Thames near Windsor. He also took with him the whereabouts of a squadron sweepstake! Before D Day, they had apparently taken bets on the time and date of the Normandy Invasion. The winner was denied his money as nobody knew where Richard Luff had left the takings!

Flying Officer Anderson RCAF, the navigator, was washed up at Calais three weeks later and is now buried in the Canadian War Cemetery on the cliffs overlooking Calais.

The remaining crew then fought to bring their stricken aircraft home, throwing out guns, ammunition, indeed anything they could remove, into the English Channel. They finally made land at 02.28am, crashing just short of the airfield at RAF Ford. When you realise that Ford is only 1/2 mile from the sea, and that they could not make it to the airfield, you begin to understand how close they came to ditching in the sea. All were uninjured. The crew were given the customary one week compassionate leave.

On the 8th of August, Baker and Bond were transferred to 570 Sqn at Harwell where they teamed up with an existing crew who had lost their pilot due to sickness. This crew were to remain together until the end. They flew another three missions to France during August and September. On a resupply drop to Arnhem on the 23rd of September, EF298 was shot down by flak killing all on board and are buried in the Arnhem Oosterbeek War Cemetery.

The crew of Short Stirling LJ440.

Left: F/Lt Richard Norman Purnell Luff DFM. Middle: Pilot, F/O William Baker. Right: F/Eng Sgt Richard Bert Bond.

LJ924 piloted by P/O D'E Minchin completed his mission but it is believed the troops jumped into a field before the D.Z.

EF309 piloted by F/Sgt Waltritch could not visually identify the D.Z. so dropped the troops on a timed run from F/C.

LJ841 piloted by F/Lt Gribble was hit by flak and was seen by most of the crews in flames east of the D.Z before crashing.

The crew was: Pilot: F/Lt Fred Gribble, Nav: F/O Alexander Edward Bothwell, F/Eng: Sgt Edward Whitehead, W/Op: F/Sgt Harry Edgar Wooton, B/A: F/Sgt Phillip Charles Goddard, A/G: F/O

Members of the British 6th Airborne prior to Operation 'Tonga'. Their role was to hold the bridges over the River Orne and the Caen Canel, Drop Zone 'N'

Sydney Frank Yardley. Gribble, an American, and his crew are the only Commonwealth Personnel buried in the Cagy Communal Cemetery, Calvados, France.

The graves of the crew of LJ841 in Cagny Communal Cemetery.

6th June: Seventeen aircraft were detailed on Operation Mallard, to tow gliders on the second wave to Normandy, with the remainder of the British 6th Airborne Division and drop them at D.Z. 'W'.

All 17 aircraft successfully released the gliders over the D.Z. encountering very light flak.

LK505 piloted by F/Sgt Hill received damage to the starboard wing and tailplane.

LJ564 piloted by F/Sgt Fordham was hit by flak while crossing the coast. The navigator and flight engineer were slightly injured after the aircraft took numerous hits.

Both LK505 and LJ564 returned to base safely.

7th June: The Airspeed Oxford piloted by P/O Light went to Ford and brought back F/O Baker and three of his crew.

8th June: Seven aircraft were detailed on a resupply operation, as part of Operation Mallard. Six crews received a recall signal when halfway to D.Z. and returned. Two landed at Ford.

LJ837 piloted by F/O Powell, his wireless operator did not receive the signal and carried on and completed the mission and returned to base safely.

9th June: Three new crews did map reading and radar training at night.

10th June: Eight aircraft were detailed to France on a resupply drop to D.Z. 'N' codenamed 'Rob Roy'. All aircraft were successful. Light flak was encountered over the D.Z.

EF234 piloted by W/O Tickner received numerous hits on the aircraft but carried out its mission and returned to base safely.

LJ924 piloted by F/Sgt Waltrich also received numerous hits including the port tyre and flap. The aircraft had to make a belly landing back at base. All the crew were safe.

11th June: Two crews on local towing

12th June: Seven crews were detailed to France, taking off from Fairford on operation 'Sunflower VI'. All carrying a mixture of troops and containers. All aircraft reported no enemy action, and all completed the drop successfully.

13th June: Five crews detailed on a special operation to France, coded 'Sunflower VII'. No enemy action was observed, and all had good and successful trips.

14th June: Twelve crews on local air test. Four crews on local towing.

15th June: Two crews on local towing.

16th June: One aircraft was detailed to France on operation 'Ballbasket. The D.Z. was reached but weather was u/s so the containers were brought back.

17th June: Six crews detailed to France on operation 'Dingson IX', carrying paras and containers. No enemy action, and all aircraft were successful.

18th June: Four crews took-off on a resupply drop from Fairford, on operation 'Townhall', carrying containers, panniers and tyres. All had good trips and were successful.

19th June: Nine crews did a three-hour cross-country.

20th June: Five crews went to Fairford for operations but returned owing to trips being cancelled.

21st June: Four crews went to Fairford for operations, three returned when mission was cancelled, and one failed to take-off due to the aircraft being u/s. This failure was due to poor staff work at Fairford.

22nd June: One aircraft dropped 18 Canadian paratroopers on Div D.Z. at 09.30hrs.

23rd June: Nine aircraft were detailed on a resupply drop to France on operation 'Townhall VIII', carrying containers and panniers. All aircraft had to fly through a balloon barrage to reach the D.Z. All were successful.

LJ843 piloted by F/Sgt Hanson had to bring 3 containers back due to starboard wing bomb doors u/s.

RAAF Aircrew in front of a Stirling taken on 4th June just before D-Day.

Front Row L-R: F/O Caldwell, P/O Light, P/O Marshall, W/O Steele, F/Sgt Stevenson, F/Sgt Prowd. Back Row: P/O D'E Minchin, F/O Thatcher, F/O Smith, F/Sgt Hoystead, Lieutenant Scott Glider Pilot, F/Sgt McLaren, W/O McCarthy, F/Sgt Mann, W/O Tickner. F/O Smith Was Killed by A V 1 Flying Bomb in the U.K. on the 30.6.1944.

24th June: One aircraft detailed to France with 24 containers. D.Z. was reached but there was no reception, so the containers were brought back.

25th to 29th June: There was truly little flying due to bad weather.

30th June: Ten aircraft were detailed to France on operation 'Townhall XX', D.Z. 'W'. Although there was heavy flak from the Caen, area all aircraft had a good trip and were successful. This ended sorties for June, the squadron flew 85 sorties with the loss of 8 aircrew and one aircraft LJ841.

The view from the astro hatch of Sgt Keith Prowd's Stirling, dropping containers on a re-supply drop after D-Day.

RAAF and British army aircrew in front of a Horsa glider

L-R Front Row, Kneeling: F/Sgt R. W. Mann, W/O Hugh Joseph Kilday, (Accidentally killed in an aircraft accident in Norway on 10 May 1945); P/O R. D'E Minchin

Standing: F/Sgt Clarence Campbell, (Lost on operations over north west Europe on 31 March 1945); Sgt J. Powell, British army glider pilot; P/O W. L. Marshall, W/O G. R. Oliver, Sgt T. Auty, British Army Glider pilot; P/O L. J. G. James
Sitting in glider doorway: F/Sgt Henry Hoysted DFC, P/O C. E. Light
Standing in doorway: Staff Sergeant Sampson, Brighton British Army Glider pilot.

Stirling ZO-W towing a glider at Netheravon before D-Day.

No.196 Squadron Short Stirling ZO-F prior to D-Day.

Waiting for the off, Short Stirlings of 196 Squadron getting ready for D-Day.

A line up of Short Stirlings at RAF Keevil.

July 1944

1st July: All aircraft returned to base from Harwell and Ford. Three others were air tested.

2nd July: One aircraft were flown on air tests.

3rd July: Two aircraft were detailed to France. Both were successful with an uneventful trip.

4th July: Eight aircraft were ordered to France on a S.O.E. operation, 'Dick92'. All aircraft were successful.

LJ925 piloted by P/O James was attacked by an aircraft thought to be friendly and was slightly damaged but no casualties.

EF234 piloted by F/O Powell, when returning over the Channel, was attacked by an enemy aircraft, there was no damage and the rear gunner returned fire and observed a strike on the aircraft.

Pilot F/O L.J.G. James

W/Op on LJ925 F/Sgt G. Bartholomew

Bomb aimer aboard LJ564
H.G. McLAREN

Pilot, F/O Cess Light

5th July: No flying today.

6th July: Five crews were detailed on a S.O.E. operation to France. All were successful.

LJ564 piloted by P/O Light, when landing at base, overshot the runway and the navigator and rear gunner were slightly injured. The aircraft was repaired and sent to H.Q. Airborne Forces.

7th July: Five aircraft were detailed for an S.O.E. operation. Four were successful, but LJ945 piloted by F/Sgt Hill, received no reception, and brought his load back to base.

8th July: Three crews were detailed on an S.O.E. operation to France. Two were successful, but LJ583 piloted by F/Sgt Green located the D.Z. by radar but there was no reception.

9th July: No flying due to weather.

10th July: Three aircraft were on an S.O.E. operation to France. Two were unsuccessful due to no reception.

11th July: Eleven aircraft detailed for an S.O.E. operation to France. One failed to take off due to a burst tyre. All aircraft encountered bad weather and visibility. Nine were successful but LJ988 piloted by W/O Tait had no reception at the D.Z.

12th July: Air to ground firing.

13th July: Two crews on a S.A.S. operation. Both were successful but were diverted to Ford on return due to bad weather at base.

14th July: Five crews on S.O.E. operation, taking off from Tarrant Rushton. Four were successful but one had no reception at D.Z.

15th and 16th July: Crews were detailed for operations but were later cancelled.

17th July: Four crews were detailed for an S.O.E. operation. All successful.

18th July: Ten aircraft were detailed on an S.O.E. operation. Six were successful.

LJ848 piloted by S/Ldr Brown had no reception and saw an enemy aircraft but it did not attack.

LJ510 piloted by P/O D'E Minchin did not locate the D.Z.

EF248 piloted by F/Sgt Fordham was unsuccessful due to Gee being u/s, and very bad weather, so returned to base and dropped his load in a rope dropping area.

19th July: Five crews detailed for operations but was later cancelled. Four crews towed Horsas loaded with personnel on postings to Harwell.

20th July: Twelve crews were detailed on an S.O.E. operation. All aircraft encountered bad weather, including an electrical storm, and poor visibility due to low cloud. Only six were successful. Of the other six, five had no reception.

LJ505 piloted by F/O James did not reach the D.Z. due to the p/o engine being u/s and the aircraft could not maintain height, so his load was jettisoned.

21st July: Twelve crews detailed for operations but was later cancelled. Some local towing.

22nd July: Eight crews did mass take-offs with Horsas.

23rd July: Nine crews were detailed on an S.A.S. operation. Seven were successful but two were not due to no reception.

LJ888 Piloted by P/O Marshall was successful, but one of the panniers chute opened inside the aircraft so was not dropped.

24th July: Three crews were on an S.O.E. operation and all were successful.

25th July: One aircraft went out on a S.A.S. operation carrying 12 troops 5 containers and 1 pannier. Because of poor reception only the troops were dropped.

26th July: Ten crews detailed for operations but later was cancelled. Crews on local flying and fighter affiliation.

27th July: Eleven crews were detailed on a S.O.E. operation. Seven was successful, the other four encountering bad weather over D.Z., so brought their loads back.

28th July: Eight aircraft detailed on a S.O.E. operation. Only three were successful. The other five encountered bad weather and were out of Gee range.

29th July: One aircraft went out on a S.O.E. operation and was successful.

30th July: Nine aircraft went out on a S.O.E. operation. Seven were successful but two brought their loads back due to no reception.

31st July: Air tests carried out. Three crews detailed for operations but were later cancelled.

This brought to an end, operations for July. The squadron had flown a total of 106 sorties with no loss of aircrew, and the loss of just one aircraft LJ564.

August 1944

1st August: Crews on local flying and air tests.

2nd August: Eleven crews were on a S.O.E operation while two other crews carried out a S.A.S. operation. The two on the S.A.S. operations encountered accurate light flak over the D.Z. One Stirling was held by searchlights, but thankfully the German flak gunner's aim was off on this occasion, no damage. Both operations were successful.

Of the other eleven, ten were successful, the other having no reception.

LJ 557 piloted by W/O Azouz was hit by flak in both starboard engines and the propeller of the outer engine fell off but he carried on and dropped his load and returned to base. For this superb act of airmanship Warrant Officer Azouz was awarded the D.F.C. This was the report in the paper.

Supplement to the London Gazette, 27 October 1944.

Air Ministry.

The King has been graciously pleased to approve the following award.

Distinguished Flying Cross.

Acting Warrant Officer Mark Azouz (1398796), R.A.F.V.R., 196 Squadron.

'One night in August, 1944, this Warrant Officer was detailed for an operation over the Brest Peninsula. In the run-in to the target, the aircraft was hit by anti-aircraft fire. The propeller and reduction gear of the starboard outer engine were shot away. The ailerons were damaged and other parts of the aircraft were struck by fragments of shell. Despite this, Warrant Officer Azouz successfully completed his mission and returned safely to base. This pilot has set a fine example of gallantry and devotion to duty'.

LJ557 ZO-H after making a forced landing at Colerne. The sortie was a bombing raid on Brest harbour where the Scharnhorst and the Gneisenau were supposed to be anchored. After a hot reception it lost both the port and starboard outer engines thus earning pilot Mark Azouz the DFC.

3rd August: One aircraft was ordered to France on a S.O.E. operation but was unsuccessful due to no reception.

4th August: Fifteen crews were detailed on a joint S.O.E. and S.A.S. operation. Of the eight S.A.S. aircraft all dropped their loads of troops and panniers. Of the seven S.O.E. aircraft, the reception was poor over the D.Z. Five were successful but two failed.

5th August: Two aircraft were detailed on a S.A.S. sortie and nine on a S.O.E.

The two on S.A.S. was not successful due to no reception.

One of them LJ440 ZO-Z piloted by P/O King, when crossing the French coast on the way out saw a Focke-Wulf 190 and fired 250 rounds at it. There was no damage to their aircraft.

Pilot: F/L C.W. King

W/O: F/Sgt D.G. Hunt

Charlie King with F/Eng: F/Sgt J.R. McGhee

LJ440 ZO-Z September 1944
Nav: F/Sgt A. Tebay, W/Op: F/Sgt D.G. Hunt, F/Eng: J.R. McGhee, A/G: F/Sgt J. Heslop in turret, Pilot: F/Lt C.W. King, A/B: F/Sgt R. Curran

LJ440 ZO-Z September 1944. L-R: King, Tebay, Curran, Hunt, Heslop, McGhee.

Stirling 7T-T, January 1945.
Back L-R: F/Eng: Sgt Pete Smith, Pilot: F/Lt Charlie King, Nav: W/O Jack Colcoran, A/B: W/O Howard McClaren, Front L-R: A/G: John Heslop, W/Op: F/O Dudley Hunt. The nose art depicts a kangaroo with the motto "IT'S IN THE BAG". On the right of the kangaroo are the tally of daggers denoting the operations carried out.

7T-K January 1945.
L-R: Charlie King, Pete Smith, Jack Colcoran, Dudley Hunt, Howard McClaren, John Heslop

Of the S.O.E. aircraft, eight were successful and one not due to no reception over the D.Z.

6th August: Six crews detailed for operations but were later cancelled.

7th August: Two aircraft detailed on a S.A.S. operation. Both were successful.

LJ494 piloted by F/Ltn Vanrenen was late over the D.Z. due to take-off being delayed due to swing.

Two aircraft also on a S.O.E. operation. One successful and one not.

8th August: Ten aircraft were detailed on a S.O.E. and S.A.S operations but one failed to take off the aircraft being u/s. All aircraft had successful trips.

LJ928 piloted by W/O Oliver saw a JU88 and the gunner fired a burst.

LK556 piloted by F/Lt Meredith also fired at an enemy aircraft over the French coast which immediately broke away out of sight.

9th August: Seven aircraft on S.A.S and S.O.E. operations. One failed to take off on the runway due to the aircraft being u/s. The two S.A.S. encountered light flak.

LJ502 piloted by W/O Holloway was coned by searchlights and hit by flak, the port tyre being damaged but made a successful landing back at base. Of the other four on S.O.E. three were successful but one had no reception.

LJ988 piloted by W/O Tait flew through light flak ten miles inland, then heavy flak over Laval, which caused slight damage to the aircraft.

10th August: Eleven aircraft was laid on for a S.O.E. operation. Two were cancelled, and one failed to take-off due to the position of the D.Z being incorrect. The other aircraft on the same target was recalled. Of the other seven one was unsuccessful due to no reception.

11th August: Six crews were laid on for a S.O.E. operation but two were cancelled. The other four had good trips and were successful.

12th August: Local towing carried out.

13th August: four crews were laid on for a S.A.S. troops drop. One was cancelled but the others all had successful trips.

14th August: Four aircraft detailed for a S.A.S. drop. All successful but LK510 piloted by P/O D'E Minchin had one paratrooper refused to jump.

15th August: Flying was cut to a minimum as the station was to prepare for a major operation.

Wing Commander Alexander flew to Group with the Station C.O. and Wing Commander Davis of 299 Squadron for a conference.

16th August: Three crews were laid on for a S.A.S. drop. Two were unsuccessful as the exact D.Z was not found. The other, LJ440 Piloted by W/O Breed, was successful but had a paratrooper who refused to jump.

17th August: Four crews on a S.A.S. troop drop. Three were successful but one had no reception.

18th August: Five aircraft laid on for a S.O.E. operation. Only two were successful, the others failed due to bad weather.

19th August: Eleven crews detailed for operations but was later cancelled.

20th August: Five crews on a S.O.E. drop. All successful and were congratulated by the A.O.C. for carrying out a good job of work under very bad weather conditions.

21st and 22nd August: Operations were cancelled due to bad weather.

23rd August: Six aircraft detailed on a S.O.E. operation. Four were successful but two failed as they hit a cold front on route.

24th August: Fifteen aircraft on a mixed S.O.E. and S.A.S. drop. Eleven were successful, the other four had trouble locating the D.Z. Special message was received from the A.O.C. at the briefing for an all-out effort in spite of weather.

25th August: Fifteen crews on a joint S.A.S. and S.O.E. operation. Only seven were successful due to bad reception.

26th August: Seven crews detailed on a S.O.E. operation. Three were successful but two had no reception.

LJ836 piloted by F/O Campbell had an engine failure on the port outer.

LJ810 piloted by S/Ldr Angell had an engine failure on the starboard outer.

27th August: Ten crews were detailed on a S.O.E. operation. Seven were successful but three had no reception.

EF311 piloted by F/O Campbell, had his port inner engine u/s over the D.Z. and was unable to feather it, and decided to drop his load although he had no reception. He flew back on 3 engines, until about 45 miles from the English Coast the port outer propeller flew off and put the port outer engine u/s. He then carried out an excellent ditch on two engines ending up about seven miles from Selsey Bill.

All the crew got into the dinghy and after about 6 hours they were seen by two fishermen, both old life-boatmen, who were out in a 13-feet out-board motorboat to re-bait their lobster pots. A fresh to strong westerly wind was blowing and the sea was rough. The fishermen were three miles west of Thorney coastguard station when they saw the airmen. They went at once to their help. With considerable difficulty they got the six men into their boat but had to abandon the rubber dinghy. With eight men on board the 13-feet boat was well loaded, and it took her an hour and a half to reach shore, as her petrol was exhausted, the men had to row. They also had to bale all the time. None of the crew were hurt. They were eventually taken to Tangmere.

28th August: Three crews on a S.O.E. drop. All successful.

EF272 piloted by F/Sgt Waltritch encountered some light flak and received some slight damage to aircraft. One aircraft went to Tangmere to pick up F/O Campbell's crew.

29th August: No flying due to weather.

30th August: Air tests carried out.

31st August: Eighteen aircraft on a S.O.E. operation. One was cancelled when it burst two tyres on take-off but there was no damage to the aircraft. Eleven were successful, but the other six were not due to bad weather. Crews on leave were recalled by 23.59 hrs.

This brought to an end the operations for August. The squadron flew a total of 154 sorties with the loss of no aircrew and one aircraft EF311.

September 1944

1st September: The squadron was getting ready for a major operation with gliders.

2nd September: Briefing for phase one of operation with Horsas. Marshalling of tugs and gliders carried out. Operation postponed at 20.00hrs.

3rd September: Tugs and gliders un-marshalled.

4th September: No flying due to bad weather.

5th September: Twelve crews detailed on a S.O.E operation to France. Eight were successful, but three had no reception.

LJ836 piloted by F/Lt Askew, when on the outward journey and over the French coast, had p/o engine failure and had to feather it. They turned back and had to jettison the load in the English Channel to retain height.

6th September: Three crews set out on a S.O.E operation to France. They encountered bad weather over the D.Z. Two were not successful due to no reception.

LJ928 Piloted by F/O Jones was successful but was fired upon by American A.A. guns. No damage was sustained.

7th September: Aircraft were marshalled for major operation with Horsas.

8th September: Seven aircraft on air tests with aircraft from pool.

9th September: Briefing for operations, 12 S.O.E. and a major operation. Major operation cancelled and aircraft were de-marshalled at 1800hrs. Of the S.O.E. operation eleven were successful but one had no reception.

10th September: Ten crews on a S.O.E drop. All crews were successful.

11th September: Nine aircraft on a S.O.E. drop to France. Six were successful but the others had no reception. S/Ldr Angell posted to 295 Squadron as Wing Commander. S/Ldr Brown took photos of aerodrome to which the Squadron may move.

12th September: Five crews to France on a S.O.E. operation. Only two successful due to no reception. F/O Arnold flew S/Ldr Angell and crew to Harwell for posting.

13th September: No flying.

14th September: Twelve crews detailed for operations but were later cancelled.

15th September: Two crews to France on a S.O.E. drop. One successful and one not.

16th September: Early in the morning the whole camp was sealed off. No one allowed in and no one allowed out. Briefing took place at 13.30hrs for major operation. The operation was to put the 1st Airbourne Division down near Arnhem, Holland. The aircraft being marshalled before dusk for take-off.

17th September: The first lift of twenty-six Stirling/Horsa combinations. Coded 'Market I'. 22 combinations successfully reached the L.Z. Of the other four all the ropes broke. Three gliders were seen to land safely and one ditched in the sea, but the crew were seen to be picked up. All tugs returned to base safely.

18th September: 'Market II', the second lift to drop the 1st Airborne Division at Arnhem. 22 Stirling /Horsa Combinations. Twenty were successful. On one the rope broke about 10 miles from L.Z. but the glider made a safe landing near target.

LJ440 piloted by P/O King had 2 hits on the aircraft from light flak but returned safely.

Of the two that failed, one glider pulled off but landed safely in England. The other got badly out of position and had to be pulled off. It appeared to blow up on hitting the water.

19th September: 'Market III', the third lift. Nine Stirling/Horsa combinations with the 1st Airbourne Division. Another 15 aircraft on a resupply drop. It was a bad day for glider towing owing to bad weather. Of the nine combinations only 5 reached their target.

LJ926 piloted by F/O Arnold encountered light and heavy flak over the L.Z. and had one hole on the port side of the fuselage.

LJ846 piloted by W/O Breed took several hits by flak over the D.Z.

LK142 piloted by F/Sgt Waltrich took hits and the bomb aimer was wounded in the leg.

Of the four that were unsuccessful, LK505 piloted by F/Sgt Hill the rope broke and the glider was not seen to land.

Pilot: F/Lt Brian Arnold with W/Op: Ken Nuttall on the left and A/B John Hibbs on the right and the ubiquitous bicycles found on every RAF station.

LJ846 piloted by F/O McComie had to cast of the glider due to an engine seizure and return to base.

LK145 piloted by F/O Jones had to abandon due to the s/o engine stuck at -2 boost. The glider was brought back to base.

LJ843 piloted by F/Sgt Green, just after take-off, the aircraft was u/s. The glider and tug landed at Benson. Of the 15 resupply aircraft 14 were successful and one was missing.

LJ894 piloted by W/O Baker had two holes in the aircraft.

LJ848 piloted by S/Ldr Brown had several strikes on his aircraft and a tyre burst on landing.

EF249 piloted by F/Sgt Campbell also received several strikes on his aircraft.

LJ 502 piloted by P/O Ellis also received several hits on the aircraft.

LK556 piloted by F/Lt Meredith encountered small arms fire over the D.Z. which put one small hole in the fuselage.

LK152 piloted by F/Sgt Pyvis took many hits over the D.Z. The army despatcher was injured. One of the aircrafts tyres also burst on landing.

EF276 piloted by P/O Carroll, when over the D.Z., was hit by light flak and had his intercom and trim tabs shot away.

LK557 piloted by W/O Azouz was badly damaged by light and heavy flak over the D.Z. but made it back to base

EF248 7T-V Piloted by W/O Prowd was missing.

The crew was Pilot: W/O Prowd, Nav: F/O Powderhill, A/G: F/O Gibbs, W/Op: P/O Wherry, F/E: Sgt Matthews, A/G: F/Sgt: Gordon. Also on board was a second Navigator: F/O Chalkley, Air

Pilot: F/Sgt C. Campbell.

W/Op: F/Sgt G.G. Allman.

F/Sgt G.A. Banfield air bomber on S/Ldr Brown's Crew.

F/Sgt L.C. Balderamos, W/Op with W/O Pyvis' crew. Leopold ("Poli") Balderamos, on leave, visiting his friend, the actress, singer, and songwriter Nadia Cattouse, also from Belize, (who had joined the ATS) at Achnasheen, in Scotland.

Mechanic 2nd Class Hooker of the HMS Daedalus, Royal Navy, who was a passenger, and two Drivers of the (Airbourne) Composite Coy RASC.

This was the first of 196 Squadron's aircraft to be lost during Operation Market Garden. At the time several members of the Royal Navy's Fleet Air Arm were flying with RAF crews to gain experience of Stirlings, however AM2 Len Hooker is not mentioned on the 'Details of Crew' and therefore his presence aboard the aircraft must be recorded as unofficial. In any case, as has been reported in a book about the Arnhem operation, Hooker was not a friend of Keith Prowd, nor was he invited aboard the aircraft by him. Prowd writes:

"Leonard Hooker was not a friend, and to my recollection I had not met nor seen him prior to 19/9/44, and even then I would have thought he was a despatcher, but I cannot really remember what he looked like, and being a despatcher he would have been cleared by either the Flight Commander or the squadron office. In Frank Chalkly's case he was cleared by the flight office. Frank was a friend and a particular friend of our navigator. Frank was the navigator for another Australian pilot. Pilots could not take passengers on flights without permission. A lot of pre-take off drills have to be observed by every crewman, and in the pilot's cockpit drill, he checks that each crew member has performed his checks prior to starting up the engines. My instructions to all personnel after check was to make sure that if they walked around the 'plane to take their parachute with them. I specifically did this to anyone, except my crew who already knew the rule.

The reason we went out that day was that a guy called Cess Light (Pilot Officer C.E. Light), who later made quite a name for life saving equipment in the surf business, couldn't go on this Tuesday, there was something wrong with their aircraft, and the commanding officer asked me if we would go. I needn't have done, as we had done our particular duty, but the boys agreed and Cess Light's navigator, Chalkley came with us, plus a couple of Matelots in the back to push out stuff, and the normal crew.

I cannot remember the route we took to Arnhem, but a very short time before the drop zone, we were hit by flak which set the outer starboard engine on fire, with smoke billowing out from it, making us an easy target. If we had had more time I would have feathered the propeller and used the anti-fire button.

Formating on our port wing was another 196 Squadron pilot (Fred Powell an Englishman), and we waved to one another just seconds before we were hit by the flak which set us on fire, and at the same moment the despatchers were pushing the containers out of the side back door. I found out after I was liberated from the POW camp, that Fred had reported that no one would get out of V-Victor as it was all smoke and flames, and no one could survive. It was not until the 50th Anniversary at Arnhem that Fred found out that some of us were still alive.

Our height at the time was 1500 feet and due to the heavy flak we also lost 2 more engines, and a Stirling doesn't fly very far on one engine. I was afraid to increase power to the engines for fear that more petrol would cause an explosion, from which no one would survive, especially at that height. Obviously, I instructed the crew to bail out. Hooker was apparently behind me near to the navigator and did not have his parachute because it was beyond the main spar where the fire was fiercest, and he had asked John Wherry if he could parachute down on his back. At about 750 feet, I was satisfied everyone had evacuated the plane and, I put my 'chute on, rushed back to the main spar called out to anyone, no answer, so I went back to the escape hatch up front and noticed the altimeter was at about 550 feet, I pulled back on the control column, then down to the hatch and noticed the ground was so close, uttered a profanity, pulled the rip cord wrapped my arms around the 'chute and jumped; while still falling I heard a very large explosion and thought it was probably V-Victor.

I landed in a pine forest, the parachute caught in a tree, released myself and stupidly buried my Mae West, but not the parachute, I then knelt down looked up to heaven and said, "What do YOU want me for?" because I really thought I should have been killed. I surveyed the situation and wandered around for quite a while, when to my surprise, I was confronted by a squad of German soldiers who lined me up against a tree. I was of the opinion I was to be shot but they searched me and then marched me off to Kleine Kweek, where I was informed of another airman in the area, and the guard took me over to him. It was Mike Powderhill who had been shot with a spray of machine gun bullets from his head to his thigh, and his private was out, so the German guard allowed me to lift his trouser and drop it back in. To me that was the defining moment for poor Mike, and at least he had a little dignity at the end." (Mr. Rap, a Dutch farmer, witnessed Powderhill's descent who, after landing in a clearing and discarding his parachute, attempted to run towards some woodland but was hit by small arms fire from German soldiers in a nearby farm.)

I did not see Leonard Hooker's body. I was not aware his body was at Kleine Kweek. Gibbs, our bomb aimer, was injured (shot at), on the way down. Both Jim Gordon and John Wherry, both of whom were wounded by rifle fire during their descent, saw him in hospital and when Germans advancing on the hospital threw a few grenades in, Reggie Gibbs was unfortunately killed. Lofty Matthews, our Canadian engineer came out on a pannier, I found out afterwards, and was found near a hotel on top of this pannier and was dead. It is presumed that he was also shot dead on the way down."

Of the RASC Despatchers, driver Chaplin died of his wounds in a German hospital on the 11th November 1944, while driver Smith is listed as missing in action and has no known grave. AM2 Hooker was the only member of the Royal Navy to be killed during Market Garden.

Prowd continues:

"We were taken to a holding area in Arnhem where I was subjected to severe questioning by a very big blond German who wanted to know if any 'planes were coming over the next day. When I failed to respond, he hit me across the face with a small Italian Beretta revolver in his hand. Believe me it hurt. He then stole my wristlet watch and signet ring, both given to me by my parents in Australia for my 21st birthday which I had in the UK. I went outside to meet up with John Wherry and Jim Gordon. If my memory serves me correctly one of them saw Reg Gibbs, and I think Lofty Matthews. We were then entrained off to Weisbaden where I was held for 3 weeks interrogation, then sent to POW camp Stalag Luft VII at Kreitsberg near Bankau (or it may have been Bankau near to Kreitsberg) some 20 miles from Cracow in Poland.

Warrant Officer Keith Prowd as a Flight Sergeant in 1943.

Then on 20 January 1945 we were assembled, packed up and sent on what has been declared 'the German Death March,' ahead of the Russian advance. We marched day and night for a couple of days with quite a few dying from cold as the temperature was about -20C and more, and we did not have any warm clothing. A lot has been written about this march. For this purpose, sufficient to say that what food we received, we stole, we ate snow and any grass we saw, we stole potatoes, dehydrated silver beet and anything else we could find. At one stage I had severe bronchitis which Dr. Morrison diagnosed as double bronchial pneumonia, and had it not been for two friends (Frank Tait and George Pringle both Queenslanders), and the only three day's rest we had on the entire march, I would not have survived. We were paraded at night and were forced to walk through a very, very severe blizzard which was very scary, and quite a few were lost in that blizzard. We lost a lot of weight. Also, we were strafed by a USA Thunderbolt aircraft when some 66 were killed.

After about 6/8 weeks of snow walking, we were entrained to Luckenwalde about 40 miles from Potsdam. I would like to mention with great respect and homage, Captain Collins, who was a Church Of England minister of religion who would walk up and down the column, (which at the beginning was about 1500 POWs), saying 'Only a few more miles fellows, keep you pecker up,' or words to that effect, he did that at least twice a day, so one does not have to be a genius to understand how the fellow POWs felt about him, and how many more miles he walked than us. Not only that, but he would always find a box to set up an altar and have a service. He was a big man, an Oxford Blue and had two of the biggest feet I have ever seen.

Keith Prowd at the controls of his Stirling.

At Luckenwalde there were 30,000 odd people, mostly Russians, Americans, and Brits some Poles and Italians. There were some scenes about obtaining wood for the fire illicitly, obtained by dismantling an unoccupied building. A visit by the Red Cross inspected us, made some recommendations but none were carried out. The food was brought to us in copper clothes washers but it was better than nothing.

We paid 1500 cigarettes for the purchase of a Lancaster Bombers radio from one of the guards, (and we also had Sergeant Shoultz, who was also a very big man but a glorious singer who had performed in the Berlin opera House). We were able to follow the advancement of the allies and Russian advances, the allies stopped at the River Elbe, which was only 40 miles away, but the Russians came our way and eventually liberated us by driving their tanks down the barbed wire fences, which also crippled the tracks and they had to stay there. The Russian commander demanded at a meeting of all pilots, that we had to go and fly their planes, which we refused to do, and as a result of our refusal he closed down the camp and reduced our food supplies. Before this incident six of us saw where there was a weakness in the wire, so we lifted the nails and walked around the forest and perimeter of the camp and mended the wire when we returned.

Keith Prowd P.O.W 1944

Then we received a visit from and American reporter who hadn't been advised of our liberation, so he said he would organised a truck to pick us up and take us to the crossing on the River Elbe. Days went by and we decided to take matters into our hands, and went to our wire corner, drew lots to go out, and when we went the last one was fired upon, but the rest of us got away. When some few miles down the road we saw an American truck approaching, so we told him of the trouble, and he hid us under the seats and filled the truck with others who had decided to leave, and after 36 hours and much procrastination by the Russians we managed to cross the Bailey Bridge at Magdeburgh where we were treated royally by the Americans. Then back to the UK via Brussels where we attended the 21 club and had a sit down meal."

Also on operations that night was P/O Chuck Hoystead in LJ922. His wireless operator, Mike 'Taffy' Simpson, recalls:

"When we were all lined up on the peri track at Keevil with our engines running, my skipper Henry 'Chuck' Hoystead always liked me to sit down by the back entrance door while we were taxiing. This was so I could lean out and look underneath the wings to tell him if there were any obstructions beneath that he couldn't see from the cockpit because of the nose being so high. I had to make sure that the main wheels stopped on the perimeter track. Right from our very first op' dropping supplies to the Resistance, I found that my intercom lead wouldn't reach the plug in the

F/O Reggie Gibbs.

F/Sgt John Wherry.

aircraft, so I had it lengthened after the first operation by adding another intercom lead to make it some 6-8ft in length.

So, I was sitting there on the taxi track when Jim Metcalfe came running up to us saying his pilot had set an engine on fire and could he come with us. I hurriedly told Chuck about it. 'Get him in,' he said. 'I can always do with another pair of eyes up front. Tell him to come up and sit in the second dicky's seat.'

Jim came to Arnhem with us and returned safely. His navigator who went with W/O Keith Prowd's crew got killed when they all had to bale out with two engines on fire, the third overheating and about to catch fire. They baled out so high they were shot to pieces in their harnesses as they floated down. Keith saw four of his crew hanging by their harnesses in the trees all shot up. Lofty Matthews, flight engineer, was seen to come out on a pannier parachute, a smaller 'chute intended for containers. He either fell off or was shot off and killed instantly. (His wife was a Canadian nurse who'd travelled to the U.K. to be with him. She arrived at Steeple Ashton the day he was killed).

Our skipper, Chuck, had been incensed by rumours passed around the station by the 'Poms' about the Aussies hanging back when it came to facing the flak. Chuck was determined that they wouldn't say it about this Aussie. The result was that when we got to Arnhem there were only two people in front of us – the wing commander and the squadron leader. Earlier that day the wing commander had insulted us, calling us pigs, and told us we would fly at 500ft, no higher, no lower. Any crew that flew above or below this height, and his number was taken, and would be out of aircrew.

We had also been told to formate in threes as much as we could to increase our firepower. One Stirling was in front of us about 400yds away, if that. One minute there were three of us, the next minute the middle one had just gone whoomph into thousands of bits. We ran the risk of flying through the debris. Luckily the explosion had blown everything out and it was just like flying

Sgt Dennis "Lofty" Matthews.

through a black hole and we emerged on the other side virtually untouched, but the fellows on the other side got damaged by bits of the aircraft. Just as two aircraft in front of us began to drop their supplies and we were about to drop ours, some aircraft from another station that had been misbriefed came in from our port quarter at right angles, 1000ft above us. Wicker baskets containing five cans of petrol each were dropped without parachutes from the aircraft, narrowly missing us. We dropped our supplies and Chuck put the Stirling into a sideslip, nearly taking the top off a church steeple. Above the noise of the engines, and although wearing a headset, I could still hear the outside the aircraft the sound of, whoomph, whoomph, whoomph, whoomph. That was the German guns on the deck. I've never forgotten it."

20th September: Seventeen aircraft took off on 'Market IV', to Arnhem on a resupply drop. Fourteen were successful but most aircraft were hit by flak.

LJ583 piloted by P/O Carroll had light flak damage in the main plane.

Pilot: P/O Ron D'E. Minchin

LJ928 piloted by F/Sgt Sargant had light flak damage in fuselage.

LJ948 piloted by F/Ltn Askew had flak damage to fuselage and wings.

EF272 piloted by F/O Jones had the s/o engine hit over the D.Z. and had to be feathered.

LJ810 piloted by F/Sgt Hancock had flak damage in port wing.

LJ894 piloted by W/Com Baker had flak damage in fuselage.

LJ925 piloted by P/O James had damage to both port and starboard inner engines.

LK510 piloted by F/O D'E Minchin had hits to fuselage and both wings.

EF318 piloted by P/O King was hit by flak, his bomb aimer was injured and had to make a forced landing at Woodbridge.

LJ988 7T-T piloted by W/O Tait was missing.

The crew was: Pilot: W/O William Robert Tait, Flight Engineer: F/Sgt. Andrew Joseph Murphy, Navigator: F/Sgt Cyril Mabbott, Bomb Aimer: W/O Ernest Walter Bancroft, Wireless Operator:

F/Sgt. Terence Bowers Cragg, Air Gunner: P/O. Donovan Walter Benning. Also on board was Air Despatcher Driver: G. Neale and Air Despatcher Driver: A. Nye.

The aircraft crashed in the grounds of the De Branding open air swimming pool, north of W. A. Scholtenhaan at Doorwerth. The Stirling got into trouble during the approach. It came in flying low over the Lower Rhine, west of the Doorwerth Castle. Maybe the crew attempted to make an emergency landing on some farmland at Boersberg, but it crashed. All of the crew, with the exception of the second air despatcher who was wounded and captured, perished in the crash. All the crew are buried in the Arnhem Oosterbeek War Cemetery.

The crew of Stirling LJ988.
L-R: W/O Bancroft, F/Sgt Mabbot, F/Sgt Cragg, W/O Tait, F/Sgt Benning, F/Sgt Murphy

A photo of five crews at Keevil in April 1944. Numbered are the crew of LJ988 No.1 Bancroft, no.2 Cragg, no.3 Mabbot, no.4 Murphy, no.5 Tait. It is believed that Benning is 1st on left centre.

LJ954 piloted by P/O Ellis successfully dropped their load but were shot up by flak. The pilot was injured, and the aircraft had to make a crash landing north of Brussels. All on board including two RASC detail were safe but the aircraft was a Write-Off.

The crew was: Pilot: P/O J.F. Ellis, Nav: F/Ltn A.E.W. Laband, A.B: F/Sgt W.J. Smith, W.O: Sgt P.F.J. Barnard, F/E: Sgt D. Noble, A.G: W/O C.H.B. Talbot. Also, of the 63rd Airbourne Div. Cpl. Jones and Driver Rhodes.

LJ840 5T-G piloted by F/Sgt Averill successfully dropped his load, but while over the D.Z. was badly hit by flak and burst into flames causing all the crew to bale out. All the crew landed safely and evaded capture. The aircraft crashing at Batenburg, Gelderland.

The Crew was: Pilot: F/Sgt J.P. Averill, Nav: F/Sgt D.B. Stevens, A.B: F/Sgt J.H. Dowsett, W.O: F/Sgt A.E. Yelland, F/E: Sgt E.F. Chandler, A/G: Sgt L.N. Haywood.

A narrative by the Flight Engineer Ted Chandler:

Day 1. Wednesday 20th September 1944 – Prepare to Bale Out.

"We had a load of 24 parachute containers, three in each wing cell and eighteen in the bomb bay, plus several large wicker baskets carried in the fuselage, along with two R.A.S.C. Despatchers.

When we were hit, I used a fire extinguisher to extinguish a fire in the main port wing, through a gap in the fuselage we had made with a hatchet. As the smoke cleared, I thought this had been successful, but the pilot said the hatches had been opened and had taken the smoke away. 'It's quite serious Ted' he said. We were still flying through the flak and the two RASC despatchers continued to drop panniers. The smell of cordite was strong, and bits of shrapnel were hitting the fuselage like rain, coming in the floor hatch opening and whizzing around the inside of the aircraft.

Luckily not one of us was hit. Meantime some flames had travelled along the insulation, which was covering the interbalance line that connected the tanks between each main plane. The pilot had feathered the port inner engine and climbed away from the main Arnhem battle area. He climbed to approximately 5000 feet on three engines, then gave the order to bale out. The navigator, bomb aimer and pilot all successfully baled out from the front hatch. From the rear hatch, the rear gunner went first, followed by the two RASC despatchers. I was still attempting to fight the fires and had stupidly disconnected my intercom for ease of movement, when the Aussie wireless operator came and told me that the others had all gone. I had to go forward to my station to pick up my 'chute so I checked that that the pilot had gone and that the auto pilot ('George',) was still operating efficiently. I then went to the rear hatch, clipped on my Irving 'chute and checked it quickly. The Australian, Allan, watched me safely away and then he followed. We landed two fields apart. We certainly did not know much about parachuting as we do now. As far as I can remember, I counted to ten before pulling my rip-cord, but Allan reckoned that my chute only just cleared the static lines guard, which was forward of the tail wheel. You were supposed to bring the safety pin handle back but goodness knows were mine went. I kept my chin well in but when the main 'chute opened, it gave me a nasty kick below, despite having a tight harness. Fortunately, it was a fine sunny day, and my descent was quite peaceful.

I started oscillating, and remembering our instruction, pulled both straps across my chest. This remedy worked very well. As I neared the ground, I thought I should make a good landing, but the last few feet came up very quickly, and I was carried to a tall hedge. The parachute draped over it and my feet were in a small ditch, one of them was quite wet. I saw Allan descending, then looked around to see what reception we were going to get. I was too busy during the last few minutes on the aircraft to even remember my revolver (and chocolate!). Allan remembered his though. I then noticed a man running towards me across a ploughed field. He was dressed in a blue denim suit, peaked cap and boots. I wondered briefly if he was a German soldier. He gesticulated up and down with his arms and shouted, 'you fly, you fly'. He was all smiles and then a whole crowd of locals came through an opening, kissing us, patting us and hanging flower garlands across our shoulders. By this time, the wireless operator Allan Yelland had joined me and received the same treatment. Different locals began pulling us to go with them and grappling amongst themselves to offer us hospitality. We were eventually taken on the back of two bicycles to a farmhouse, were we were given a cooked meal. Two hours later, we were introduced to a resistance patrol who were going to lead us to an army patrol if possible. Before going, they asked if we were injured. I had a kick from the harness and wondered if I had a rupture, so they took me to a doctor who examined me. He said that there was no permanent damage and that it was probably just a strained muscle which would not cause too much trouble. All the time he was asking me questions, about reference units and how many there were. I evaded direct questions, but was not sure if he was just curious, as the locals had taken me to him, or if there was a more sinister reason for all these questions. However, I mentioned the incident in my debriefing when we arrived back at Keevil.

F/Sgt Yelland and I were then told that the resistance group would help us to make contact with the British Army (30 Corps) who were pushing their way to Nijmegan. We either walked or were given a lift on the back of a bicycle. After a while we boarded a reasonable sized rowing boat and started moving down a river (possibly the Waal, although there were three rivers on the map). We had gone some distance when we thought we were being fired at. We kept low, then went ashore and carried the boat along the riverbank for approximately 300 yards, quite cautiously. We were then back on the river and moved some distance. I cannot remember all the details but I believe we crossed a second river. After a while we were in contact with an army officer in a scout car. His radio was crackling out with garbled messages and he did not seem too pleased to meet us. He said, "you can hear that lot, it's is very difficult here at this time. You two can come along with

Two photographs of Flight Sergeant Peter Averill.

WOP/AG F/Sgt Allan Yelland

The crew of Sgt Peter Averill in happier times.

Flight Engineer Sgt. Ted Chandler

Standing at the rear exit door, the crew of Sgt Averill. 1st on the right is Flight Engineer Ted Chandler.

Navigator F/Sgt. Dennis Stevens

us but I cannot guarantee that you will meet the rest of your crew. There are a lots of you chaps around about." After an hour or more, we eventually did make contact with the rest of our crew. We were in a small town which our pilot believes was Battenburg, however I thought it had a different name. We visited the Burgomaster's office and all signed the visitor's book.

We also met a couple of aircrew, who had baled out of a Dakotas. One had very thoughtfully kept his parachute to sleep in that night. We had let the villagers keep ours. We were then in the charge of the army (Gen. Horrocks, 30 Corps) and were practically on the front line. Although we were mostly NCO's, the RAF aircrews were invited to stay with the army officers that night. We enjoyed a meal with them and had some wine. I shared a bottle with a major, who said 'Drink the wine you will sleep better for it tonight.'

I do not remember having too many blankets where we were attempting to sleep, however, I did get some sleep, although the gun-fire seemed non-stop all night long. I was probably also thinking how lucky we had all been to escape serious injury. (That may be with hindsight, as we have all realized over the years how lucky we were.)"

Day 2 – Thursday 21st September 1944.

"Early morning, there was a lot of activity amongst our armoured units. They were getting ready for a local scouting/reccy. When they realised we were returning to the U.K., they wrote odd letters and cards and asked us to hand-deliver or post them. This was against regulations but I think we were quite diplomatic with our deliveries. There were two for pubs in the East end of London. As I came from this area, I delivered them personally when I returned, and I was toasted several times by all the regulars. When the armoured vehicles returned from their sorties, they had Nazi helmets hanging from their vehicles, some had obviously been taken in battles, and some of them were quite new. I took one of the newer ones home. However my Mother never liked it and when my father died tragically, she threw the helmet away. At this time, we had lost contact with our two army despatchers but understood that they would not return to the U.K. with us, they were to be seconded to an army unit. We were still being looked after by the army and my flying boots were beginning to become uncomfortable, so I asked a group of army chaps if they would be willing to exchange them for a pair of army boots. This group contained several war correspondents and they raced away, probably to the quartermaster's store, and one of them came back with a brand new pair of boots and exchanged them for my flying boots. We then travelled in an Army lorry to Eindhoven. There were several halts along the way to allow some Canadian sappers to come through with their amphibious ducks, which were being used to rescue what was left of the 1st Airbourne. We also encountered several German snipers, who stopped our passage until they were dealt with. In most cases, the 101st and 82nd U.S. Airbourne units were keeping the road open for us. We eventually reached Eindhoven which had only just been liberated in the last few hours. Eindhoven should really have been called 'Phillips City', as in later life having worked for the Phillips Company, I have learned how much they helped the resistance prior to liberation. We entered the railway station and the American troops were going crazy, looting all the parcels waiting to be posted and seemingly not caring whether they were booby-trapped or not. I saw packs of newspapers and a stack of Nazi published magazines called Signal. On the front was a picture of a flying bomb being despatched to England. I took a copy and had it for several years till it got mislaid. From Eindhoven, we travelled to another transit camp to stay for the night. Nearby, villagers were celebrating their liberation with coloured lights and illuminated plaques, showing loyalty to Queen Wilhelmina."

Wireless Operator Allan Yelland. *Bomb Aimer Jonny Dowsett.* *Rear Gunner Bert Phelps.*

Day 3 – Friday 22nd September 1944

"We were now on our way to Brussels. The army was still driving us in a 10cwt scout car. When we had stopped in one village with the canvas drawn open, some villagers looked in, saw the blue uniforms and thought we were German prisoners. They threw a few stones at us and a couple spat at our pilot who was nearest, he quickly drew his revolver and dispersed them. We reached Brussels late in the afternoon and were booked into an old monastery which the army had taken over. We were to sleep there for the night but they allowed us a pass to visit Brussels during the evening. As we were walking round the streets, an army MP asked me why I was not wearing my forage cap. I was a bit cheeky to him and said something about leaving it 200miles back. I think he understood and let me pass without reporting me. We found a nice dance hall and I was able to dance quite well in my new army boots."

Day 4 – Saturday 23rd September 1944

"This was our fourth day away from Keevil and it seemed a lot longer. We were taken to Brussels Airport, to await our turn for an air passage to England. A few hours later, we boarded an RAF Dakota, complete with nursing orderlies and were flown to Broadwell. At Broadwell, we were received by a most efficient Adjutant, our first encounter with a female WAAF Adjutant! She phoned our Adjutant F/Lt Welman (who was quite elderly), to inform him of our arrival. Due to the bad communications, this was the first news they had had of us, since we had gone missing. She said that he was overcome with the good news of our return. He laid on a Stirling for our immediate return to Keevil, which was flown by F/Sgt Hancock whose crew were also pleased to see us".

LK556 7T-Y piloted by F/O McOmie was irreparably damaged when hit by flak and the supplies caught fire. The flight engineer and the two air despatcher's baled out. The aircraft eventually crash landed between Elst and Valburg. The crew survived the crash and evaded capture eventually made their way back to Keevil.

The flight engineer and the two despatcher's bodies were found dead in a field in Elst and are buried in the Jonkerbosch War Cemetery Nijmegen.

P/O Walter Marshall   *W/O Joe McCarthy*   *F/O D. Smith who flew with Marshall's crew in June before being transferred*

The crew of LK556 was: Pilot: F/O J.W. Mcomie, Nav: F/O J.L. Patterson, B/A: F/O G.M. Cairns, W/O: F/Sgt R. Brooks, F/Eng: Sgt D.N. Clough, A/G: F/O G.F. Talbot.

LJ947 piloted by P/O Marshall after dropping his load was hit by flak. The blast injured both the pilot and bomb aimer, and also rendered both port engines u/s. The aircraft crash landed near Brussels. All the crew were safe.

The crew of LJ947 was Pilot: P/O W.L. Marshall, Nav: Sgt L.A. Benson, B/A: P/O G.H. Tole, W/O: W/O J.F. McCarthy, F/Eng: Sgt W. Pyatt, A/G: F/Sgt F.L. Hatchett.

LJ851 7T-E piloted by W/O Oliver was shot down by flak before reaching the D.Z.

The crew of LJ 851 was: Pilot: W/O G.R. Oliver, Nav: F/Sgt J. Oates, B/A: F/O C.H. Henderson, W/O: W/O F.L. Steele, F/Eng: F/Sgt D.E. Royston, A/G: W/O L.G. Gelinas.

W/O G.R Oliver seen here looking out of the cockpit of LJ841 7T-E 'E for Elephant'.

A narrative by the flight engineer Dennis Royston:

"We flew to the Arnhem area towing Horsa gliders on the 17 & 18 September 1944, packed with members of the Airborne Division and their equipment. Due to tragic shortage of aircraft on the 19th we were rested, but on the 20 September we set off with our bomb bays full of parachute canister supplies and two parachute panniers in the fuselage to be dispatched by two army dispatchers at the appropriate time. We were on course and dropping fairly fast on our run in towards our DZ when!!! Crump – we had been hit and the port wing between the engines was on fire. The port wing was dropping, and the skipper had little control over it. He ordered crash positions and with considerable skill coaxed it down to within a few feet of the deck when he uttered an unprintable mouthful followed by 'the wing has dropped off'. This saved the fire from spreading to the fuselage. There was a lurch, a loud scraping sound and the nose filled with turnips. We were down, not far from Eindhoven and no-one was injured – not a scratch between us. We were soon out of the astrodome and scanning the horizon. Our Canadian rear gunner had drawn his .38 and using choice words invited the Jerries to do their worst. Skipper told him to put the bloody thing away. We decided to make for a wood, about half a mile away, for cover, but hearing shouting we thought we had been spotted and hit the deck. We stayed down – peering occasionally in the direction of the shouting, until we could see men running towards us with their rifles held above their heads. We sensed they were ours. We were taken back to their field HQ at Westerhoven where they informed us that the wood was seething with Jerries they had chased there half an hour ago and were expecting a counter attack.

Pilot W/O George Oliver

While we were being feted with tea and fags, Field Marshall Montgomery went down the main road in his staff car distributing cartons of 200 cigarettes. The sergeant gathered some of his men and said they were going to see if they could salvage our cargo otherwise blow it up as they didn't intend to leave it for them bastards. We didn't hear any explosions from the direction of our beloved 'E' Elephant, and they cheered us up by telling us that we were carrying Nitro and Mortars.

They supplied us with a driver and truck and eventually, after much diving in and out of ditches, we arrived at the Belgian village of Veerle, where we were wined and dined by a charming couple and their three daughters in their pub, and so to bed. The next morning after breakfast we had a hard job preserving our dignity as the daughters wanted all we owned as souvenirs. We ultimately arrived at Diest aerodrome where we boarded an ancient Sparrow with some wounded and flown to Brussels. There we were told to lose ourselves as they had too many wounded stretcher cases to get back – but in due course we were

F/Sgt Jimmy Oates.   *W/O Les Steele with a friend at Keevil 1944.*

delivered back to Keevil in an Anson with some walking wounded, where there was some jubilation as we were the second crew to return to the field after being missing."

A further narrative by Pilot George Oliver:

"The first day, the things I recall mainly are the fighters, the fighter cover we had, it was tremendous to see the fighters diving around the place, and we noticed several of them gunning anything suspicious they saw on the ground. Another thing I noticed was that a lot of the ground was flooded in Holland. I understand the Germans probably did this. We got our glider there all right, dropped it and did not run into any serious trouble that day. It was a highly successful venture I guess. The second day, I can't recall a great deal about the second day, we took this glider across and we did not get into problems, there was quite some flak but we were not hit. We got back unscathed. We were fairly pleased with our effort, not knowing of course the tragedy that the whole show was to become.

The third day of course we were not so lucky, we took off with a cargo of mortar bombs and also we had in the rear two army despatchers and big containers of fuel, we went over the channel, flew north across Belgium and entered Holland. We were just south of Eindhoven somewhere, when we were surrounded by flak, nothing happened for a minute or two, suddenly there was a hell of a bang, just as though a horse had kicked the aircraft. It was a tremendous bang. It seemed to be on the port side to me, but I checked the instruments and the engines were running all right, the controls were ok at that time, so we continued on, a little later I noticed that the wing was losing lift and dropping away, I did not say anything to the crew, I just trimmed the aircraft and kept my eye on everything, but it kept getting worse and worse and dropping away, I could not understand what was wrong out there.

Then a little later, I think it was Les Steele who said 'skip, we can smell fire down here'. I think it was about this particular time I began to realise there was something terribly wrong out on the port side and the wing was really giving me trouble. Eventually the fire broke through, at that time the wing was becoming so seriously inclined to drop I realized I was in serious trouble. I realised the old girl was going to let us down, I had to do something. I decided to go down, I did not like my chance of climbing away, I called the crew into crash positions, selected a field and down we went. We did not have time to jettison so we took our full bomb-bay of mortar bombs and petrol

W/Op: W/O Les Steele.

down. I did a wheels up crash landing, managed to kick right rudder on to get up the wounded wing, we slithered along. I recall the burning wing hit a tree and some of it snapped off and this may have prevented any of the fire to spread. Eventually we stopped much to our relief. We had some duties to perform, destroying documents etc. and of course I had to turn off some switches, I can't remember the details. I know we did not waste too much time, I went out of the hatch above my seat, and I was not the first. When I came out some of the others where there, standing on the ground.

I seem to recall there were some explosions, we moved away from the aircraft of course, fairly rapidly because it was burning. We moved down somewhere along a field and found a ditch. We went down in this ditch to gather our thoughts together and check our documents, I remember Junior, as he was a bit of a hard case, got his revolver out of his pouch and stood looking over the top of the ditch with this thing. I did not fancy any Germans taking us on with our Smith & Wesson's. While in this ditch we had some maps and we had a bit of a round table where we were and Jimmy Oates, of course, was able to give us a pretty good idea of where we were. It was somewhere near a village called Westerhoven, we thought we might go south, that seemed to be the logic thing to do. I don't know how far we proceeded but we were in a ditch again and saw some soldiers in the distance, we did not know if it were British or Germans, I remember junior waving his S&W again which did not appeal to me much, but as they got close they put their rifles horizontal over their head as they walked towards us, we realised then they were British. They told us the village of Westerhoven had just been taken the previous night, so we headed towards Westerhoven, well all the villagers came out to see us, we must have shaken hands with every Dutch we saw along a couple of miles. An army HQ was set up there, we were able to find a radio operator and we asked if he could send a message back to England tell them that we were safe.

We were assured that they would do so, however I found out later the message never got through. One of the things I recall in this village was that there were some artillery guns along the perimeter of the village, they were firing away, the village people were just having a look over this, just wandering around these guns firing. We went up to the army HQ, and waited there, eventually an officer gave us a map and asked what we wanted to do. I said we wanted to go back to England, he gave us a map and later on in the afternoon a light army truck arrived, we crawled aboard and set off. Heading towards Diest. We were fortunate enough to be taken in by an inn keeper, they really looked after us, they gave us a good meal, and we were amazed of the quantity of the food available. We spent the night there and next morning we began looking around for a lift further on. There was a field dressing station nearby and we were told we may be able to get a lift to Brussels. So we went out of the field dressing station and got a lift in an ambulance airplane down to Brussels and we spent the night there. In the morning, I think it was Friday morning, we decided to look around for a lift back to England. We had plenty of competition, but we got a lift on an Avro Anson, which was carrying blood plasma across. So we piled on board and we were dropped off at Keevil. We got out at Keevil and everyone was flabbergasted, they thought we were dead and gone. That night the old adjutant was very kind to me, PA Wellman, an old WW1 adjutant, always treated me as a son. He was pleased to see us. I phoned my wife, after that we had a meal and then went up to the Duke, including the army despatchers, I'm afraid we had a few drinks that night. Next day we retrieved our kits which were packed up and put in something we used to call the morgue, the kits of the missing crews were there. Geoff Bartholomy packed mine up, I had asked Geoff to write to my mother in the event of me being killed. We were given some leave, and I went to my wife."

Poor quality photograph with Cyril on the right, next to entry and escape hatch of Stirling 'E' Elephant. Four ground staff who serviced the aircraft did a magnificent job, Cyril painted the elephant emblem on the nose. The ground staff took as much pride in the aircraft as the crew did. The three aircrew are Dennis Royston (left in door) George Oliver (right in door) and Chuck Henderson, 1944.

A narrative from an eyewitness on the ground:

"On Wednesday 20th September, our village escaped from a disaster. At about 15.00 hrs allied airplanes came over again, now from the south over the forest. We saw that one of them had an engine on fire. The pilot tried to put the aircraft to the ground, he chose the open terrain between 'de Donk', 'de Mozik' and the village. This emergency landing would have been a success if he would not have touched a big oak tree with the tip of his wing. The tree broke off the wing and the aircraft turned half a circle and it slithered sideways for about 50 yards and stopped in 'de Kleine Beerze', the aircraft was burning and lay over a ditch. All of the crew left the airplane. A while later the British soldiers who were in the village brought the crew to safety. Some days later they returned to England. The Stirling had been on its way to Arnhem, to supply the troops. It carried light ammunition, mortar bombs, food and fuel. All was packed in containers, the containers carried a light and battery, so it must have been used in the dark too.

Our cows, which were in the same field as the Stirling, took off because of the sounds of the exploding ammunition. We had to go look for them in the village that evening. Also we noticed that the milking buckets and stools were burned. Our fence was damaged, so the wreck attracted lots of playing children. There was no barbed wire so we had to use the wire used by the British, it was difficult to bend this steel wire. The ammunition was a danger for everybody. My brother had found a mortar grenade and had placed it on a fire, then went into the ditch and waited for the loud bang. Nothing happened, so they went back to work. Just when they were on the other end of the field it exploded with a loud bang. Nobody was hurt. Two of the engines were in the ditch so we decided to bring all of the wreckage to the scrapyard, we used the steel armoured plates though, to make ploughing scissors, and we also used a metal frame attached to the back of the airplane. We drove 30 times to the scrapyard before all was gone. The mortar bombs, about 60, were destroyed by the British."

21st September: Ten aircraft took off on 'Market V' on a resupply drop.

Sergeant Peter Alcock in front of LJ928 ZO-L. The Alcock's crew flew many times in LJ928 including three trips to Arnhem on the 17th, 18th and 20th September. On the 21st they were rested and LJ928 was taken up by F/Sgt Ron Waltrich and was shot down killing all of the crew

Six aircraft, LJ949, LJ583, LJ272, J945, LJ505 and LJ848 were all successful, but LJ848 was hit by a falling parachute over the D.Z.

LJ502 piloted by P/O Hoystead, before crossing the English Channel, the rear gunner collapsed and had to return to base.

LJ843 ZO-R piloted by F/Sgt Green was shot down.

The crew was: Pilot: F/Sgt Charles Richard John Green, Nav: F/Sgt Richard Glyn Phillips, B/A: F/Sgt Leonard Marsh, W/Op: F/Sgt Robert Cowan, F/Eng: F/Sgt David John Allaway, A/G: F/Sgt Donald Hay Grant.

The aircraft was shot down by flak, and crashed north of Oranje Nassau's Oord at Wageningen at 12.55 h. There were no survivors, and all six of the crew and the two despatchers were recovered from the wreckage and were buried by local Air Raid Wardens in the Onder de Bomen General Cemetery at Renkum. All of the casualties were re-interred to Arnhem Oosterbeek War Cemetery on 24 August 1945.

Memorial to LJ928 behind the Rehoboth School in Doorwerth

LJ928 ZO-L piloted by F/Sgt Waltrich was shot down.

The crew was: Pilot: F/Sgt. Ronald Eric George Waltrich, F/Eng: Sgt. Leslie Victor Ratcliffe, Nav: F/Sgt. Robert Walter Forrest, B/A: F/Sgt. Stanley Arthur Leonard Townsend, W/Op: F/Sgt. Francis Ormson, A/G: F/Sgt. Sidney John Poole, Air Despatcher L/Cpl S. Law, Air Despatcher Drv. W.H. Brook.

While nearing the D.Z. LJ928 encountered an enemy aircraft and was shot down at 15.15hrs at Heveadorp (van der Molanallee), Holland. All the crew are buried in the Arnhem Oosterbeek War Cemetery.

LJ810 ZO-B piloted by W/O Azouz DFC was shot down.

The crew was: Pilot: W/O Mark Azouz DFC, W/O F/Sgt H.A. Turner, Nav: F/Sgt. G.D. Greenwell, B/A: F/Sgt. L. Hartman, W/O: F/Sgt. J. McQuiggan, A/G: F/Sgt. Peter Harold Bode, Air Despatcher Drv. A. Norton RASC, Air Despatcher L/Cpl Day RASC.

LJ810 had been hit by flak on the way into the D.Z. They successfully dropped their load but were attacked by several FW 190s who raked the plane which ended up going down.

A Narrative by F/Sgt Bert Turner:

"On the Thursday, 21st September 1944, Mark and Ginger's (Greenwell) DFC were promulgated and Mark's promotion to Pilot Officer. We were told to do an extra trip... we had done 30 on the Tuesday. (In fact today was 'Yom Kippur', the Jewish Day of Atonement). Their Group Captain asked them to do one more last sortie as so many crews had not returned the previous days and the airborne men fighting in Holland were in desperate need for supplies. Mark Azouz, consulted Leo Hartman, both were of the Jewish faith, and the other crew members, and it was decided to fly another sortie.

Groupie came to the aircraft and wished us luck, we got in, started up, but couldn't get the revs and boost on one of the engines. It was no good, it didn't matter what Chiefie did, so we had to swap aircraft and take the spare.

We climbed into the spare, and we were 20-25 minutes late. Off we went, we cut every corner we could think of, but we were still late over the target, and just as we were coming in the other lads were coming out. They had taken a battering. There were Stirlings lying all over the place, but the skipper put the nose down and in we went.

A beautiful colour painting was made to commemorate Mark Azouz, proudly wearing his DFC, who died at the age of 22. Like many other young men, he had a bright future ahead once the war was over. Like so many he paid the ultimate price for the freedom of others.

We took a battering, we had two airbourne bods with us dropping these panniers. Mac McQuiggan was down the back supervising the panniers going out and I was 'second dickie' with the skipper. We turned round and came out of it, and we were in a mess. We wouldn't get home, there was no question and the skipper asked Ginger for a course to Brussels. I had got a piece of flak of some kind in my ankle but otherwise there was nothing wrong with me, everybody was all right and everybody sounded off.

Leo came from the nose and went second dickie, and I went back to my panel. McQuiggan came from the back of the aircraft and looked like he was covered in blood. Not just spots or bits or pieces, but all over ....blood! I remember saying to him: 'For God's sake Mac, where have you been hit'. He turned round and said: 'The Elsan' (chemical toilet). Apparently a shell had burst underneath the Elsan mounting, throwing the Elsan up in the air, and all the Elsanal fluid had gone over poor McQuiggan! Is that what they call being dropped in the muck?

Back: Mark Azouz and Peter Bode. Front: Ginger Greenwell and Bert Turner.

Mark Azouz and crew.
Front Row L-R: W/O Mark Azouz, Sgt Bert Turner, F/Sgt Jack 'Mac' McQuiggan
Back Row L-R: F/Sgt Ginger Greenwell, F/Sgt Roper (not in Arnhem crew), F/Sgt Peter Bode, F/Sgt Leo Hartman.

I stuck my head out of the astrodome and when I turned round, I said to the skipper, 'we're all right now, skipper there is our escort....' I thought them to be Tempests and to this day I don't know how I made the mistake.....they turned out to be Fw 190s. They made a Vic attack from astern, whether they were sprog pilots I will never know. We couldn't corkscrew or anything, we just had to sit there, take it and get out. Pete, the rear gunner opened up and he got the man up point. Then they got nasty, they raked us. God, they gave us a hammering, where had all the dust come from? I can see it now, it was just like a fog in the aircraft, dust and muck. I remember we were diving and I was suspended in the fuselage, just standing on nothing.

Then the skipper gave the order to get out. As I went down the back, I checked on Pete, but he was dead. McQuiggan didn't want to jump because he thought his parachute wouldn't open because of the Elsanal fluid but he had to go and that was it, out he went and I followed him out through the parachute exit.

Just as I went out, I remembered the chain broke that held the exit door up, and it slammed behind me. Luckily the two of us got out all right from the back and Ginger jumped from the front exit. I opened my parachute and a voice shouted. 'Move over in the sky, I haven't got enough room!' It was Ginger Greenwell and we shook hands on the way down".

Mark Azouz, had kept the aircraft on a southerly course, giving his crew and the two R.A.S.C. despatchers the chance to bale out.

Azouz who had put the aircraft on automatic pilot went back put his parachute on and baled out. Descending under his parachute Azouz was now a single target for the German pilots who had seen their leader being shot down by the rear gunner. Mark Azouz was shot to bits while floating to earth.

The stricken aircraft, which Azouz had left on 'George' the automatic pilot, glided down onto farmland near Niftrik, an eyewitness seeing its propellers plough up the ground - one of the wings hit a row of pollard-willow and sheared off the aircraft, so too the engines which rolled on. The wreckage came to a standstill not far from the front of Schebbelaar Farmhouse. Inside the rear turret - shattered by cannon fire - lay Bode's body.

F/Sgt Peter Bode.

Sgt Bert Turner while training to be a flight engineer.

Navigator George Douglas 'Ginger' Greenwell.

The remainder of the crew, including the two R.A.S.C. air despatchers, made successful descents.

A narrative by F/Sgt Leo Hartman:

"After I baled out, I landed by a farm near Wijchen, spraining my ankle. The farmers took me in and a little later a member of the underground arrived and took my parachute and Mae West and later brought two padres. He said he saw five bale out of my aircraft.

The two padres took me to a house where I met F/Sgt McQuiggan and L/Cpl Day of the RASC, and a rear gunner from 620 Sqn, who was badly injured. A recce car arrived, and I met up with F/Sgt Greenwell and Sgt Turner of my crew. We were taken to Grave, where we left the wounded gunner, and on to 30 Corps H.Q. and then home."

Peter Harold Bode was originally buried in a field at Niftrik, his remains were moved to Wijchen Roman Catholic Cemetery after the war, where he rests alongside another R.A.F. Arnhem casualty, Flight Sergeant W. H. Skewes. Mark Azouz, being Jewish was buried in The Jonkerbosch War Cemetery, Nijmegen.

22nd September: Thirteen aircraft were loaded and marshalled but did not take-off. Four members of P/O Marshall's crew arrived back after having crash landed north of Brussels. F/Ltn Laband

and 3 members of P/O Ellis' crew arrived back after crash landing north of Brussels. W/O Oliver, crew and despatchers arrived back by Anson from Brussels, having crash landed south of Eindhoven 20/9/44.

23rd September: Thirteen crews on re-supply drop 'Market VI', including four new crews, replacements in 'B' Flight. This was the first flying these crews had done with the squadron. All thirteen crews successfully dropped their loads over the D.Z. Four aircraft had Small Arms or light flak damage.

LJ894 piloted by F/O Powell was hit by flak and his port tyre was punctured.

LK557 piloted by F/Sgt Hill was hit in the bomb doors and two panniers were jammed and were dropped wide of the D.Z.

EF272 piloted by P/O Godden was hit by flak in the nose and mid fuselage and the bomb aimer W/O Steinhauer was injured.

Crew of EF272: Pilot: P/O G.R. Godden, Nav: F/O E. Levitan, A/B: W/O A.R. Steinhauer, W/Op: Sgt W.F.M Spiller, F/Eng: Sgt W.W. Winters, A/G: F/Sgt B.G. Fisher.

Pilot Russ Godden recalls:

"All thirteen aircraft for the operation were loaded with 24 containers and 4 panniers for the encircled army at Arnhem, and parked nose to tail in two lines on the runway when we were taken out to board. My crew was supplemented by a British army R.A.S.C. private, to help in sliding the panniers out through the hinged door in the fuselage floor.

On opening the throttles for take-off the aircraft swung badly, but I was able to straighten up and take-off on the grass. An uneventful flight across in line. The 'old hands' cut the corner at a turn to form in line and we were left at the end. As a country lad I recall my surprise at the density of housing and the tiny fields as we crossed Belgium, with ribbon housing along roads linking villages, also the stacks of drying peat blocks beside the trenches from which they had been cut.

Strait and level flight at about 800ft at the bomb aimer's direction was required for the drop, and the short time involved seemed inordinately long before he released the load, with rifle/machine gun fire, and A/A shrapnel rattling like stones on a tin roof.

Pilot Graham Russell Godden

Russ Godden at his wedding to Edith with his best man, F/Eng Bill Winters.

The bomb aimer was seriously wounded by a bullet in the buttocks as he rolled over to rise after the release (that bullet creased the pitot head fairing but fortunately did not affect the speed reading). The army soldier had his thigh shattered by a half inch square piece of shrapnel, which I saw by his bedside when I visited him in Trowbridge Hospital. There were, I think, three other holes in the aircraft, including a punctured oil tank, which fortunately was self-sealing, else the port inner engine would have seized when there was no oil left. Compared with some we got off lightly.

On release of the load, I immediately dived and we crossed the Rhine at high speed (for a Stirling) and low level. The rear gunner fired a burst at a machine gun post by the river. After all these

The wreckage of LJ810 ZO-B near the Schebbeleer farm. Note the rear gun turret which was shot up by the Me109's gunfire

years I still feel emotional when I think of a Dutch group by a farmhouse as we flew past just above the trees. They were waving wildly to us in greeting. A little later I had to climb to go over a power transmission line. The low level was in case of fighter attack. The wounded men would not accept a shot of morphine, though obviously in great pain, and on approaching base I called up to advise their presence on board. It seemed I had hardly switched off in the parking bay when there was a doctor beside me. I was most impressed, and the lads presumably got their morphine then."

LK147 piloted by F/O Norton was hit by flak over D.Z. The p/o propeller flew off. The flight engineer was injured, and the aircraft had to land at Manston.

LJ949 ZO-U piloted by F/O Sparks was hit by flak over D.Z. The aircraft had to make a crash landing near Leende, Holland. The pilot and wireless operator were injured, but all survived.

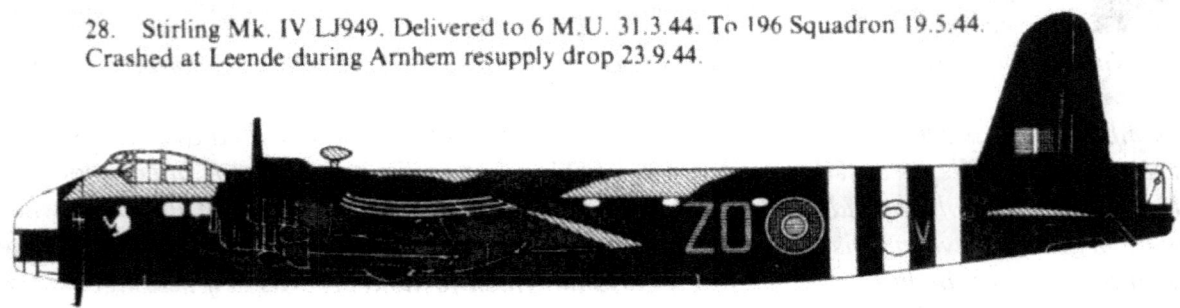

28. Stirling Mk. IV LJ949. Delivered to 6 M.U. 31.3.44. To 196 Squadron 19.5.44. Crashed at Leende during Arnhem resupply drop 23.9.44.

P/O King flew an Oxford to Wroughton to collect P/O Marshall who was discharged from hospital after crash landing in Belgium. F/Sgt Averill and crew were collected from Broadwell where they landed from Brussels.

24th September: Three crews, all new to the squadron, were laid on for a supply drop. One aircraft failed to take-off due to the aircraft being u/s.

LJ835 piloted by F/O Staines was successful.

LK142 5T-A piloted by F/Sgt Draper crashed at Spinecourt, France on supply dropping run.

The crew was: Pilot: F/Sgt D.Draper, Nav: F/Sgt Crampson, B/A: F/Sgt C.A. Williamson, W/Op: Sgt G.D.F. Kerton, F/Eng: Sgt J.C. Turreff, A/G: F/Sgt J.H. Williamson.

It is believed the altimeter had not been reset to the air pressure of the D.Z. and the pilot initiated a descent before the D.Z. had been positively identified. The aircraft was flown into high ground because it was off track and the crew was confused by some contradictory information given at the pre-flight briefing.

The A/G: Cedric Alfred Williamson, W/Op: Sgt Gerald Desmond Patrick Kerton and the F/Eng: Sgt James Campbell Turreff were all killed. They are all buried in the Choloy Cemetery in France.

The rest of the crew evaded capture and eventually returned to base in a Dakota.

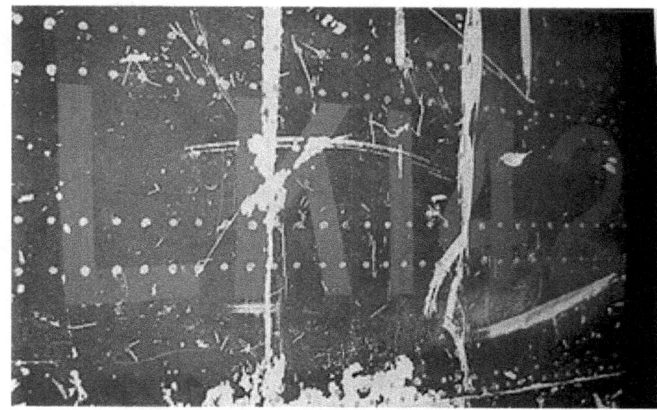 

Part of the fuselage found in France being used as a horse stable. The fuselage of LK142 is on display at the Musée du Terrain D'aviation in Vraux, France

25th September: An aircraft and crew were ferried to Great Dunmow to retrieve aircraft 'K' which was forced down with engine trouble.

26th September: An aircraft and crew were ferried to Benson to retrieve aircraft 5T-S which was forced down with engine trouble. Today, heard the first news of F/O McOmie (who was missing on 20/9/44), through the medium of The Daily Telegraph, in a story from one of their correspondents. *'I was four days behind enemy lines'*.

27th September: F/O D'E Minchin flew to Down Ampney to collect F/O McOmie who had landed there on return from Brussels.

28th September: Three aircraft were detailed on a S.O.E. operation to France. One successful, the other two had no reception.

29th September: One aircraft was detailed on a S.A.S operation to France, which was unsuccessful due to bad weather and no reception.

30th September: Nine crews were detailed on a S.O.E. to Belgium. All had good trips and were successful.

Two commanders flew to Wethersfield to allocate offices for the forthcoming move of the squadron from Keevil.

This brought to an end, operations for September. Without doubt the most costly in the squadron's history. The squadron flew a total of 155 sorties with the loss of 12 aircraft, EF248, LJ810, LJ840, LJ843, LJ851, LJ928, LJ947, LJ949, LJ954, LJ988, LK142 and LK556, with the loss of 28 aircrew.

Bomb Aimer, F/Sgt D.J. Goldberg   *W/Op: F/Sgt G.W. Sommer*

October 1944

1st October: Five aircraft were detailed for S.O.E. operations. Two encountered very poor conditions while making the sea crossing and were down to 500 feet, but both were successful and when leaving the enemy coast, they encountered heavy flak. The other three on a different D.Z. ran into exceptionally low cloud over the D.Z. and there was no reception so brought their loads back.

2nd October: Five crews towed gliders to Wethersfield containing station equipment.

3rd October: Six new crews were put on practice forming up route and container drop. Not much of a show. Obviously, new crews need squadron training before becoming operationally fit.

P/O King was flying the Oxford on the milk run to Wethersfield today.

4th October: Six crews towed Horsas to Wethersfield. Seven new crews did practice forming up route and container drop. Greatly improved on previous day.

S/Ldr Brown retrieved a glider which cast off on route to Wethersfield.

5th October: Five more gliders towed to Wethersfield.

6th October: Five more gliders towed to Wethersfield.

7th October: More gliders towed to Wethersfield.

8th October: No flying due to bad weather.

9th October: Today the squadron moved all serviceable aircraft to Wethersfield. Unable to take-off till 12.00hrs due to weather, which was unsuitable for glider towing, 29 aircraft were ferried containing aircrew and personal kit. Main party travelled by road and rail. Move well in hand. Squadron offices and billets quite satisfactory.

10th October: Six aircraft returned to Keevil for gliders. Squadron unpacking and generally settling into new quarters. Road party and personnel with private cars arrive.

11th October: Leave was restarted. 6 crews off on privilege leave.

Squadron now ready to operate tonight.

12th October: Five gliders were brought from Keevil.

13th October: More gliders brought from Keevil. Squadron has not been called on for operations.

14th October: Two new crews on night cross country. EF318 was retrieved from Woodbridge.

15th October: More Horsas brought from Keevil. 3 new crews on night cross country.

16th October: Weather once again poor. Four aircraft detailed for S.A.S. operations. Only one was successful. Two had no reception and LK193 piloted by F/Sgt Fordham had to return early due to Gee u/s. and lost air position.

These were the first operation flown from Wethersfield.

17th to the 21st October: No flying due to adverse weather.

22nd October: Four crews on local towing. One crew flew to Tilstock carrying F/Ltn Askew and crew who have now been screened. One aircraft flew to Keevil carrying crews to retrieve two other aircraft that were left behind. Seven tugs ferried Horsas from Greenham Common to Down Ampney, Blakehill Farm and Great Dunmow. Gliders were not ready at Greenham Common. Then weather closed in so tugs returned to base.

23rd October: Weather unsuitable all day.

24th October: Two crews on local flying to get their hand in after crash landing on Operation Market.

Four crews on operations. Three on S.O.E. and one on S.A.S. All were unsuccessful due to bad weather and no reception. Three landed away from base.

25th October: Four crews on local towing. One aircraft to Keevil taking another crew to pick up 5T-C. The crews who landed away last night returned to base.

26th and 27th October: Some aircraft on local towing.

28th October: One crew flew another crew to Keevil to pick up 5T-D.

Three aircraft were detailed on operations, one was u/s and did not take-off. The other two were successful.

29th October: Exercise Essex took place today. 16 crews taking part. One glider cast off and landed on a road and another landed at Keevil. All the rest were successful. Four operations were laid on but were cancelled during the afternoon.

30th October: Six crews did local towing.

31st October: Four crews did local towing. Two cross –country runs with Horsas. One Horsa was retrieved from Greenham Common.

This brought to an end operations for October.

The squadron flew a total of 15 sorties with no loss of aircraft or aircrew.

November 1944

1st November: Crews undertook local towing and air tests.

2nd November: Crews did local towing and cross country with Horsas.

Four crews were detailed on a S.O.E. operations. The crews encountered accurate light flak but received no damage. Three were successful and one not due to bad weather over the D.Z. and no reception.

3rd November: No flying due to bad weather.

4th November: Some cross country was flown with Horsas and also air tests. Three crews went to Keevil to retrieve aircraft which were left behind on move.

Six crews on A.S.R. Search but nothing was sighted.

5th November: No flying due to bad weather.

6th November: Station exercise No.1. Ten crews from squadron towed Horsas and released same in flights of 4 at base.

7th November: Local towing and air tests. One crew flew to Keevil to retrieve a Horsa.

8th November: Local towing and air tests.

Eight crews were detailed on S.O.E. operations. Seven to Holland and one to Norway. All crews experienced trouble with icing. Only two were successful. Four were unsuccessful due to no reception. The one to Norway returned early due to bad weather and engine trouble due to icing.

EF234 ZO-P piloted by F/O Norton was missing. The aircraft failed to return from Dutch operation 'Draughts 7A'. The D.Z. was at Venhuizen in the Province of Noors-Holland on the west bank of the Zuider Zee. There is no indication what happened to this aircraft, it is believed it crashed in to the North Sea and the crew was never found.

The crew was: Pilot: F/O John Anthony Norton, Nav: F/O Derek William Eves, A/B: F/Sgt Harry Ruston, W/Op: Sgt John Vass Thompson, F/Eng: F/Sgt Charles Alf Myers, A/G: Sgt Maurice Arthur Goult. All the crew are remembered on The Runnymede Memorial.

9th November: Local towing and night flying carried out.

10th November: Fifteen crews took part in Station Exercise II, towing Horsas. Gliders were released in flights of six. First time squadron has tried towing in formation of Vic of three.

11th -15th November: Crews did some local towing and cross-country exercises.

16th November: Nine new crews on group exercise with paratroopers. Troops collected at Chilbolton and exercise carried out from there. In spite of some indifferent weather at base and Chilbolton a fair standard was maintained by crews throughout the exercise.

17th November: No flying due to bad weather.

18th November: One aircraft and two crews went to Manston to collect aircraft 'Q'. However, 'Q' still u/s. Crews returned to base.

19th November: Weather unfit again for flying.

20th to 24th November: Some local towing, air tests etc. were carried out but the weather was very poor.

25th November: One aircraft to Manston to collect aircraft 'Z' which landed there during Arnhem operation. One sortie exchange of aircraft with 'Rivenhall'. Ten crews on Station Exercise III with quite good results.

26th November: Some local towing.

27th November: Ten squadron Stirling/Horsa combinations on small exercise to give S.A.S. troops air experience in Horsas.

Six crews detailed on a S.O.E. operation to Norway. Four were successful. One had no reception due to bad weather.

LJ 643 piloted by F/O King had to return early due to the s/o engine u/s and jettisoned his load and fuel on return.

On return to base all aircraft encountered bad weather in the form of extremely heavy rain. One aircraft landed away from base.

28th November: Weather unfit for flying.

29th November: Eight crews on paratroop exercise. Troops emplaned at Tarrant Rushton and drop on div. D.Z. Netheravon. Exercise appeared quite successful.

Six crews on night flying exercise. Seventeen lifts carried out. Best night flying to date at this Station.

30th November: Some local towing and night flying carried out.

This brought to an end, operations for November. The squadron flew 24 sorties with the loss of 6 aircrew and one aircraft, LJ234.

December 1944

1st December: Three crews ferried gliders to Gosfield.

2nd December: 5T-A ferried to Bourne and another aircraft to Bourne to pick up 5T-A's crew.

3rd and 4th December: No flying due to bad weather.

5th December: Crews on local towing and cross country.

6th December: Crews on local towing and some night flying.

7th December: Ten crews took part in group exercise 'Recurrent'.

8th December: Crews did local towing and some night flying.

Short Stirling Mk IV PW410 of 196 Squadron on approach.

9th December: Crews on local towing and local flying testing S.B.A. (Standard Blind Approach.) and 'George' etc. One crew to Keevil and return. Three bombing practice and formation flying.

10th December: Three crews tested the S.B.A. equipment and three crews did formation flying.

11th December: One crew was flown to Keevil in the Oxford to bring back 'N' which had been there for a few days with a burst tyre. Local towing and night flying.

12th December: One crew to Tilstock and then a cross country and some local towing.

13th December: No flying due to bad weather.

14th December: One S.B.A. test and eight air tests. Weather was still very bad.

15th December: Seven air tests and three S.B.A. tests.

16th December: No flying due to bad weather.

17th December: Local towing and air tests.

Two crews detailed on S.O.E operation, both were unsuccessful due to no reception.

18th December: Crews on night flying and local towing.

19th to 22nd December: No flying due to bad weather.

23rd December: Some local towing and air tests.

24th December: Local towing and air tests. Thirteen crews standing by for operations over Xmas.

25th December: Twelve crews ready for take-off at 08.00 hours on daylight ferrying of troops to battle front. Take-off was delayed two or three times and it was finally decided to marshall the aircraft by 10.00 hours. At 12.00 hours operation cancelled for 24hours. Aircraft de-marshalled.

26th December: Repeat of day before.

27th December: Weather unfit and operation cancelled.

28th December: Seven crews were laid on. One on S.A.S and six on S.O.E. Three were to Norway of which two were successful.

LJ643 piloted by F/Lt Merrideth had to return early due to the w/t burnt out. The other four were to Holland. Two were successful. One take-off was delayed due to aircraft being u/s which may account for no reception.

LJ502 piloted by F/O Ellis, was unsuccessful due to enemy action at D.Z. and the starboard main plane was hit by light flak.

29th December: Some air tests and formation flying were carried out.

30th December: Night flying, cross country and local towing carried out.

31st December: The squadron held a mass take-off. Fourteen crews. Stirling/Horsa combinations. Only ten managed to get off due to u/s aircraft. Bad show.

This brought to an end, operations for December. The squadron flew 9 sorties with no loss of aircrew or aircraft.

January 1945

1st January: Crews on local flying and local towing.

2nd January: Two air tests flown and three aircraft on formation flying.

3rd January: Four crews were laid on for operations but were cancelled. Weather unfit for flying.

4th January: Crews on local towing, four on bombing details and crews on night flying.

5th January: One aircraft to Northolt to collect crew where they had gone to collect 5T-X. Unfortunately, the Hun got there first, ground strafing, and wrote off 5T-X.

6th January: Weather unfit for flying.

7th January: Three crews on local towing. Weather poor.

8th and 9th January: Weather unfit for flying – snowing.

10th to 12th January: Runway u/s – snow. Aircrew clearing runways.

13th January: Aerodrome declared u/s for flying.

14th January: Twenty six aircraft flown to RAF Gosfield, and sixteen gliders. Squadron aircrew flying from Gosfield but living at Wethersfield.

15th January: Five more aircraft flown to Gosfield.

16th January: Weather unfit for flying.

17th January: Cross country and local towing carried out.

18th January: Local towing, cross country and bombing practice.

19th January: Six details of bombing carried out.

20th January: Crews on bombing and cross country and local towing.

21st January: Same as yesterday.

22nd January: Air tests carried out.

23rd January: Weather unfit for flying.

24th to 26th January: No flying. Preparing to move to Shepherds Grove. Aircrew and kit moved by road. All settled in at Shepherds Grove.

27th January: Seven aircraft from Gosfield to Shepherds Grove.

28th January: Another seven aircraft from Gosfield to Shepherds Grove.

29th January: Twenty nine aircraft from Wethersfield and Gosfield to Shepherds Grove.

30th January: The squadron now have most of the aircraft at Shepherd Grove, some u/s aircraft left at Gosfield and Wethersfield. No flying today. Stand down – Weather unfit for flying. N.B. Ready to operate from here tomorrow.

31st January: Weather unfit for flying.

No operations were flown in January.

February 1945

'Chuck' Hoysted and crew, photo taken in 1944. L-R F/Sgt Ray Owen, bomb aimer, F/Sgt Mike 'Taffy' Stimson, wireless operator, F/O 'Chuck' Hoystead DFC RAAF, pilot, F/Sgt Jack Hooker, air gunner, F/Sgt John Barker, navigator, kneeling in front Sgt Bill Garretts, flight engineer.

1st February: First operational tactical night bombing carried out. Group Captain Troop accompanied F/O Hoystead (R.A.A.F.) on this operation.

Five crews detailed to bomb Grevenbroich. All aircraft carrying 24 – 500lbs bombs.

Although encountering thick cloud on route and light flak at the target, four crews were successful.

LJ643 piloted by F/Lt Meredith had to return early due to Gee u/s. Jettisoned bombs in the area.

2nd February: Weather unfit for flying.

3rd February: Training continued. Mainly formation. Night flights carried out.

F/O Henry (Chuck) Hoystead DFC.   *Chuck with his take on Per Ardua Ad Astra, Aspro being an old headache powder.*

4rd February: Eight aircraft on tactical bombing to Grevenbroich, Germany. All good trips and successful.

5th February: Bombing practice carried out. Four night glider lifts.

6th February: Limited flying. Weather u/s.

7th February: Twelve aircraft detailed for tactical bombing of Uedem, Germany. One failed to take-off due to aircraft being u/s.

Ten successfully bombed the target.

LJ870 piloted by F/O Torrens saw a jet-propelled fighter 30 miles from target.

LJ876 piloted by F/Lt Powell, the rev counter was u/s on the starboard inner engine.

LK147 piloted by F/O Sparks had aileron trouble which affected starboard turns.

LJ926 piloted by F/Sgt Averill was unsuccessful and returned early due to Gee being u/s. Bombs were jettisoned.

8th February: Limited flying due to operational crews resting.

9th February: Varied day training continued.

10th February: Day training – timing exercises

11th February: Limited flying due to inclement weather.

12th February: General stand down due to inclement weather.

13th February: Training continued. Night towing and cross country.

14th February: Eight aircraft detailed for tactical bombing of Isselburg, Germany, carrying 18-500lb bombs. One failed to take-off due to radar failure.

Although the target was covered by cloud all aircraft were successful.

15th February: Bombing exercise laid on but weather u/s over range.

16th February: No flying due to bad weather.

17th February: Limited flying due to weather.

No.196 Squadron bombing section late 1944.

18th February: Low stratus cloud prevented morning flying. Training in timing flights in afternoon together with glider towing. Trips in gliders arranged for 24 A.T.C. cadets.

19th February: Limited flying due to weather. Operations cancelled.

LJ870 on exercise landed to fast in bad visibility with starboard outer feathered and inner not giving full power which caused the aircraft to swing, and the undercarriage collapsed, writing off the aircraft. All crew were un-injured.

20th February: Glider exercise to be witnessed by A/C/M Tedder. Three planes took off and three were cancelled due to strong cross winds. First three carried on O.K.

Nine aircraft detailed on a S.O.E. operation to Norway. One failed to take-off due to aircraft being u/s.

Three were unsuccessful due to no reception at D.Z.

EF318 piloted by F/Ltn Vanrenen saw a flak ship in Oslo Fjord.

21st February: Eight crews and one spare briefed for tactical bombing to Rees, Germany carrying 24- 500lb bombs. Nine took-off of which eight were successful.

A narrative by F/O Downie who piloted LK256 'I-Ivor' on the raid to Rees:

"The take-off, the first we had done with such a heavy load as 24 x500lb bombs, was frightening in the extreme. After the breaks were released the aircraft hardly seemed to move. I felt that its tyres were so compressed they were behaving like the wheel on a wheelbarrow being pushed through a muddy field. Everything was slower than usual, and the end of the runway was just under the nose as the needle crept to minimum speed for take-off. The controls felt much heavier than usual.

Tension built up as we crossed into Belgium, and then we spotted flak, a single stream of tracer. The odd thing was that its arc remained unchanged, and we turned away. Had some Oberleutnant or gunner fallen asleep, his finger resting on a firing button? We shall never know, but I still wonder. Rees was completely covered in cloud, and why we dropped some bombs on a field near the Rhine is probably intriguing a few aged residents even to this day."

LK126 piloted by F/Lt Campbell on return to base when making his final approach, was shot upon by an intruder. The aircraft was set on fire as it made its final approach, but the pilot brought the blazing machine down on the runway safely. As the fire took hold, its crew scrambled clear. Only one man, the rear gunner, Canadian W/O John Bruce McGovern failed to escape and was burnt to death, he is buried in the Brookwood Military Cemetery, Surrey.

Warrant Officer John Bruce McGovern RCAF.

It was never fully established but it is thought that the intruder was a JU88.

LJ894 piloted by W/Cdr Baker was shot down and crashed near De Rips, Holland

The crew was: Pilot: W/Cdr M.W.L. Baker, Nav: F/Lt G.W. Fairhall, A/B: P/O A. Evans, W/Op: F/Sgt R. Butler, F/Eng: F/Sgt H.A. Turner, A/G: F/Sgt J.R. Gordon.

It was reported that LJ894 could have been shot down by flak, but it was also reported it could have been a night fighter. Also, there is speculation that the aircraft could have been shot down by Canadian flak.

Rear gunner F/Sgt John R. Gordon was severely injured. The pilot ordered the crew to bale out and decided to make a force landing to save the life of his rear gunner. Unfortunately, both were killed in the crash landing. The other crew members who baled-out landed in liberated Holland and were safe.

W/Cdr Maurice William L'isle la Valette Baker and F/Sgt John Robert Gordon are buried in The Mierlo War Cemetery, Holland.

22nd February: Seven aircraft were detailed on a supply drop to Norway. Only two aircraft were successful, the others had no reception at their D.Zs. All aircraft were diverted to Lossiemouth on return.

23rd February: Low stratus and frost covered base. Crews returning from Lossiemouth were forced to land with cloud bas 300 – 500ft.

24th February: Local day flying only. Nine operational crews briefed for Norway but all night flights were cancelled. Weather u/s.

25th February: Five crews briefed for operation to Norway. Weather was very poor en – route. Three aircraft were successful.

Seen her at her dispersal, Short Stirling Mk.IV 7T-P

LJ988 piloted by F/Sgt Graff did not reach the D.Z. due to the starboard inner engine u/s. The load was dropped in the sea and it took the aircraft five hours to return on three engines.

LJ925 ZO-J piloted by F/O Tickner was shot down.

The crew was: Pilot: F/O Russell George Tickner, Nav: W/O Rolf W. Mann, A/B: F/O John H.D. Caldwell, W/Op: W/O Joseph Daglish Stevenson, F/Eng: F/Sgt George Alfred Humphrey, A/G: P/O Eric S. Quirk.

Tickner and his crew set out in the early evening on an operational flight to Norway. Their objective was to resupply a Norwegian resistance group near Navarsgard. Soon after crossing the border, Tickner's aircraft was attacked by three German night fighters from Kjevik airport near Kristiansand. After a brief struggle, the Stirling's starboard wing was in flames and the aircraft was beyond salvation.

Directly in his path was the town of Arendal. Tickner ordered his crew to bale out, and several managed to do so.

Rear gunner Quirk put on his parachute and kicked out the emergency exit, fortunately the flames were on the other side of the 'plane. An icy wind turns against him as he jumped out and disappears into the night. A violent jerk of the parachute says he's saved. Quirk lands on Slettebakken on Hisøy. He gets rid of his parachute and hides it in the snow. He is perplexed what to do and spends the night shivering in the shelter of a stone. He is confident that the Germans would find him, but in the morning, he is found and taken care of by the fisherman Edward Wallentinsen. Wallentinsen hides Quirk in an empty house close to his home. Here he stayed a week. More or less on his own. Quirk is then taken to Grimstad-edge, where he comes in contact with the home front. There he is

Above: Pilot Jonny Graf, 2nd from right, with his crew and 7T-P.
Below: Jonny Graf and crew and ground crew

Pilot: F/O Russell George Tickner.　　*Nav: F/Sgt R.W. Mann.*　　*BA: F/O J.H. Caldwell.*

provided with new clothes and false papers, and then he's transported to Arendal, where he goes into hiding. Towards the end of the war, he was staying in a cabin in Milorg-Fyresdal, until the Germans capitulated on 8 May. In June, he travelled back to England. Navigator Mann and bomb aimer Caldwell, baled out, but were caught by the Germans and became P.O.W.s.

Tickner aimed his aircraft for Lake Hølen, which was covered with winter ice. The stricken Stirling hit the frozen surface of the water with a violent crash after an unsuccessful attempt at an emergency landing. Ice and snow and burning debris being thrown around. Tickner, his wireless operator Stevenson, and his flight engineer Humphrey, whose parachute had been caught on the aircraft as he baled out, were killed in the crash. A large black roaring hole in the ice marked the crash site.

The bodies of Joe Stevenson and George Humphrey were recovered and are buried in The Arendal Hogedal Cemetery. Russ Tickner was killed at his controls and disappeared under the lake were his body remains. He is remembered on The Runnymede Memorial.

26th February: There was some local day and night flying. Wing Commander Turner arrived to take over the squadron.

27th February: The station undertook a glider towing exercise with 20 combinations. Night towing, 17 lifts. Exercise Frigid (paratroopers) laid on but cancelled due to strong winds.

28th February: The flying was mainly by new crews ferrying gliders from Gosfield. No night flying programme.

This brought to an end, operations for February. The squadron flew 60 sorties and lost 6 aircrew and 4 aircraft, LK126, LJ870, LJ894 and LJ925.

W/Op: F/Sgt J.D. Stevenson. *F/Eng: F/Sgt George Humphrey.* *A/G: F/Sgt E.S. Quirk.*

The crew of Stirling LJ925.

Back L-R: John Caldwell, Rolf Mann, George Humphrey, Eric Quirk
Front: Russ Tickner, Joe Stevenson.

Rolf Mann and George Humphreys.

Memorial at the crash site.

A twisted metal hub from LJ925.

March 1945

1st March: Limited programme. One cross country by day and two by night. Briefing for Station glider exercise to take place tomorrow. Squadron Leader Taplin arrived to take control of 'B' Flight.

2nd March: Station glider exercise took place with 12 combinations. Limited other flying.

Five crews were briefed for supply drop to Norway. Three were successful but one had no reception.

The other, LJ979 piloted by F/Lt Meredith had to turn back as his instrument panel and artificial horizon was u/s.

3rd March: Training programme day and night. Cross country and local towing.

4th to 6th March: The training programme continued.

7th March: Station Glider Exercise took place.

8th March: The training programme continued. Two aircraft detailed on a S.O.E. sortie to Norway. One successful, the other not due to no reception.

9th March: Mainly practice formation flying for day programme. Five new crews with screened pilots carried out paratrooper night drop exercise.

10th March: Bombing practice carried out during day.

Two aircraft from the squadron, but one manned by a 299 Squadron crew carried out exercise Ibrox (French Alps). Both successful.

LK242 ZO-A piloted by W/O Brown of 299 Squadron were lucky to survive when a crate was being dropped, the strop guard, (a forked bar suspended below the tail to keep the parachute line clear of the tail wheel), struck the top of a mountain. Although damaged the aircraft returned to Shepherds Grove safely.

11th March: Cross country training by night.

12th March: Station glider exercise. Night cross country.

Two Stirlings over the French Alps. No.196 Squadron's ZO-A is in the bottom photo.

13th March: Some air to air and air to ground firing carried out.

14th March: Exercise Vulture. Good glider exercise. 19 aircraft took part from this squadron.

15th March: Training programme continued. Special glider operational exercise. Two aircraft on astro cross country.

16th March: Training programme continued after mid-day due to weather. Four aircraft on astro cross country at night. Three on night cross country without radar aids.

17th March: Training programme continued. Special glider operational exercise. Two aircraft from squadron took part.

18th March: Training programme continued. Four aircraft on night flying cross country.

19th March: Low stratus cloud. Flying programme cancelled.

20th to 22nd March: No flying except for air tests.

23rd March: Briefing before Operation Varsity.

24th March: The squadron took part in Operation Varsity Airborne Rhine Crossings. Operation to land airborne troops in the Wesel area of Germany by glider. The squadron sent 30 aircraft and crew as part of several thousand aircraft, it was the largest airborne operation in history to be conducted on a single day and in one location. Out of the thirty, six were unsuccessful.

LJ835 piloted by F/Lt Arnolds tug rope broke.

LJ931 piloted by F/Lt Brown in the slipstream the glider broke loose.

LK345 piloted by F/Lt Spruell in the slipstream the glider broke loose.

LK147 piloted by F/O Breed the glider air pressure was nil and requested return.

LK193 piloted by W/O Fordham the glider pulled off over Rhine with no reason.

EF318 piloted by F/Sgt Catterall, the glider cast off with no reason.

All the rest of the crews had good successful trips apart from LJ838 and LJ979.

LJ838 piloted by F/Ltn Campbell completed their mission on three engines and had to land at Brussels.

Operation Varsity, 'The Rhine Crossing, March 23rd 1945. Photo taken by F/Sgt Bunny Mason, rear gunner. The photo shows the crew and the Horsa en-route to the Rhine. Tug pilot, F/O Russ Godden

LJ979 7T-F piloted by F/Ltn Vanrenen completed their mission but was hit by flak on turn for home and crash landed near Overloon in Holland.

LJ979 crew was: Pilot F/Ltn Henry Poleman Vanrenen, Nav: W/O Reginald Bert Tammas, A/B: W/O Douglas Handley, W/Op: W/O John Edward Chalk, F/Eng: F/Sgt John Holmes, A/G: P/O John Leonard Jones.

A narration by F/Eng John 'Sherlock' Holmes.

"The glider had just been cast off and the skipper turned for home. Then there were a couple of loud explosions and F for Freddie seemed to bounce up and down, we had been hit by flak. One burst hit the nose were the bomb aimer lays. Then a second hit the underneath of the fuselage just behind where the cockpit is. Fortunately, Blondy (Handley the bomb aimer) was then riding second dickie. Chalky (Chalk the wireless operator) was stood behind and in the middle of the two pilot's seats. He took most of the blast in his legs. The skipper was also hit in the legs and both he and Chalky were badly hurt. Tam (Tammas, the navigator) who had also been slightly injured in the leg by some shrapnel, and I, helped Chalky back down the plane and were joined by Jonah (Jones the rear gunner). I went back to my control panel and it was obvious two of the engines were out. The skipper also said he had lost most of the hydraulics. It was obvious we were going down. There

Back L-R: Jack Chalk, D. Crosby, John Holmes, Len Jones
Front L-R: Reg Tammas, Henry Vanrenen, Doug Handley.

Henry Poleman Vanrenen DFC. *John Holmes while training.* *Len Jones and his rear turret.*

was no chance of baling out as we were too low. The skipper told us to take crash positions. Just before we were about to belly land, I turned off all fuel supplies to the engines. The skipper brought the old kite down into a ploughed field with absolute precision, a textbook belly landing, although being in a pretty bad way, he was always Mr. Cool personified.

We helped the injured guys out of the plane and made our way over to a wall and sat down against it. We had no idea where we had come down, whether in Germany or Holland. Although lying in agony Vanrenen, drawing his service pistol, said, 'men if the Germans come, we will defend ourselves'. We all looked at each other in astonishment, and I don't know who, but someone said, 'If the bloody Germans come skip we are bloody surrendering'. Thankfully, he agreed.

In a very short time, we were surrounded by people. They were all hugging and kissing us. We had obviously made it back over into Holland and all the locals from the nearby village had run to help us. Also, within no time at all an army medical truck had seen us come down and made their way to us. They took Vanrenen and Chalk away to an Army Medical Unit.

The rest of us were taken to the village which was called Overloon. We spent the rest of the day and night in the village and were treated like Kings. The next day we made our way to Tilburg were we boarded a Dakota back to England."

LK197 was piloted by P/O I.A. Downie.

Downie recalls:

"The crossing of the Rhine seemed to me the culmination of four and a half years of preparation. Rumour on the airfield was that the complete plans of The Rhine Crossing Operation were in German hands, and that we should prepare for massive resistance. Instead, the operation was

John Holmes.   *Jack Chalk with 'Patch' the crew's mascot'.*   *Len Jones.*

Len Jones while in training.   *Chalk, Holmes and Tammas the day before 'Operation Varsity'.*   *Doug Handley.*

LJ979 with the villagers of Overloon.

Tammas, Holmes, Jones and Handley sat on the wing of LJ979 with one of the Alders family in whose field they crashed.

Handley and Tammas with LJ979.

A commemorative plaque where LJ979 crashed landed in a field of the Alders family farm

magnificent. We had a front row view – armchair comfort – feeling of being on the winning side at last.

On the morning of the 24th March, 196 Squadron seemed tuned to give its maximum performance. Every Stirling that could, flew that day. Gliders were parked on either side of the runway, angled to preserve precious runway length. There was little wind when we boarded 'E-Easy'. The sun started to light the scene, the air was clear, cloud slight and high, as we sat awaiting the signal to start engines. All was in such strange contrast to the danger, destruction, disaster and death that we were to affect that day.

I pressed the start buttons and my Hercules' whined, coughed and grumbled into life. The plane in front was only halfway down the runway when my throttles were fully open, and my bomb aimer, Lou Schaverien, had clamped them tight. It seemed an age before I could feel the glider becoming airborne, but soon 'wheels up' was given. We circled, cutting the corner until we were in formation, following the leaders to the south coast. It was only as we flew on that the realisation came to us of the immensity of the operation. Our squadron was soon joined from port and starboard by others knitting into a fast-expanding stream. Altitude was low, somewhere near 1,800 ft. The stream soon stretched to the horizon. Halfway across France dots appeared on the port side – aircraft returning from the Rhine. It was an amazing site, overshadowing all the westerns I had seen.

Lou Schevarien of P/O Downie's crew

We crossed the Rhine, and map reading became more intensive as the bomb aimer and navigator kept us exactly on course. I had already worked out my tactics for getting out of what might be a tricky situation. We released the glider at 500 ft., which seemed an extremely dangerous altitude in view of ack-ack firing from small arms on the ground. I went into a climbing turn for home, viewing the continuous stream of aircraft arriving. We were halfway back across France before we passed the end of the stream. Over the Channel we dropped our towrope. The Scots member of our crew felt it a great waste – surely a farmer or fisherman could have benefited from it?"

Jonny Graf Piloting EF276 recalls:

"It was a beautiful day, the air was so fresh, the sky so blue. The stream of 'matchboxes' (gliders) stretched two by two like animals heading for the Ark, ahead as far as the eyes could see. We were flying Stirling Mk. IV 7T-L. It had Hercules Mk. XVIs on which fuel-air mixture regulation was achieved automatically by reference to throttle setting. At +2 p.s.i. boost economical cruising was obtained. The setting of +6 p.s.i. provided climb conditions or was useful for limited combat periods. Intermediate settings were prohibited since they would have brought rich mixture jets into operation, playing havoc with fuel consumption. '7T-L' had seen more youthful days, (It had been delivered to the Squadron in late 1943) and towed with rather less zest than many others. At maximum cruising boost it was able to maintain station, but not altitude. I proceeded by a series of hops, which must have wearied the glider. Over the intercom wired through the towrope we wished the glider crew well, and they released on time. By then the ground was strewn with gliders.

At low altitude the air seemed full of them losing height and jockeying on to their approaches to landing. Above the air was full of tugs, now lightened of their trailing loads, banking and turning away trailing empty towropes."

25th March: Crews on standby for resupply drop if necessary. (Not carried out).

26th March: Local flying only.

27th March: Training programme re-commenced.

28th March: Stand-down. Weather u/s.

29th March: Training programme continued.

30th March: Day training programme continued.

Six crews briefed for operations to Norway, only one successful.

LK320 piloted by F/O Sparks had to return early due to port outer engine failure and icing.

LK146 piloted by F/O Jones was tracked by an enemy fighter and on the second attack the aircraft was damaged but made it back to base.

LJ988 piloted by F/Sgt Graf was attacked by an enemy fighter and had the hydraulics and IFF shot away. He also made it back to base.

LJ888 ZO-T piloted by F/Sgt Catterall was attacked by enemy aircraft and was missing.

The crew was: Pilot: F/Sgt Derrick Vivian Catterall, Nav: F/Sgt George Sidney Reed, A/B: F/Sgt Reginald Sergius Paul Harding-Klimanek, W/Op: F/Sgt Thomas Louitt Brunton, 22, F/Eng: Sgt Paul Montefiore Myers, A/G: F/Sgt John Richard Cross.

LJ 888 which took off for a highly secret operation planned for a special equipment drop for the Norwegian resistance movement (Milorg), in order to obtain information as to the German progress with the development of the atomic bomb at the heavy water plant at the town of Rjukan in Telemark. The code name for this operation was 'Snaffle 6' - only the pilot and navigator were told of the target, the dropping zone and the type of the equipment carried. This was a Special Operations Executive mission.

LJ888 took off at approx. 21.30hrs for S.E. Norway for the dropping zone BIT (59.20N - 09.56E), with 10 containers and 12 packets. On the night of the operation, it was a brilliant moonlit night with no cloud cover and the aircraft was an easy target for the German JU 88s who had superior speed and armament. The JU88s were armed with 20mm cannons and the Stirlings only had 7mm Browning's, which were no match, and the speed of the Stirlings was 190mph against the JUs 300mph, which clearly indicates that they were sitting targets without a chance. Furthermore, the Germans had located a radar station at Risor and a night fighter station at Kristiansundon the south east coast of Norway. LJ 888 was shot down over Arendal with the loss of the whole crew. All the crew were buried in a communal grave in Arendal Cemetery.

LK197 piloted by F/O Campbell was missing.

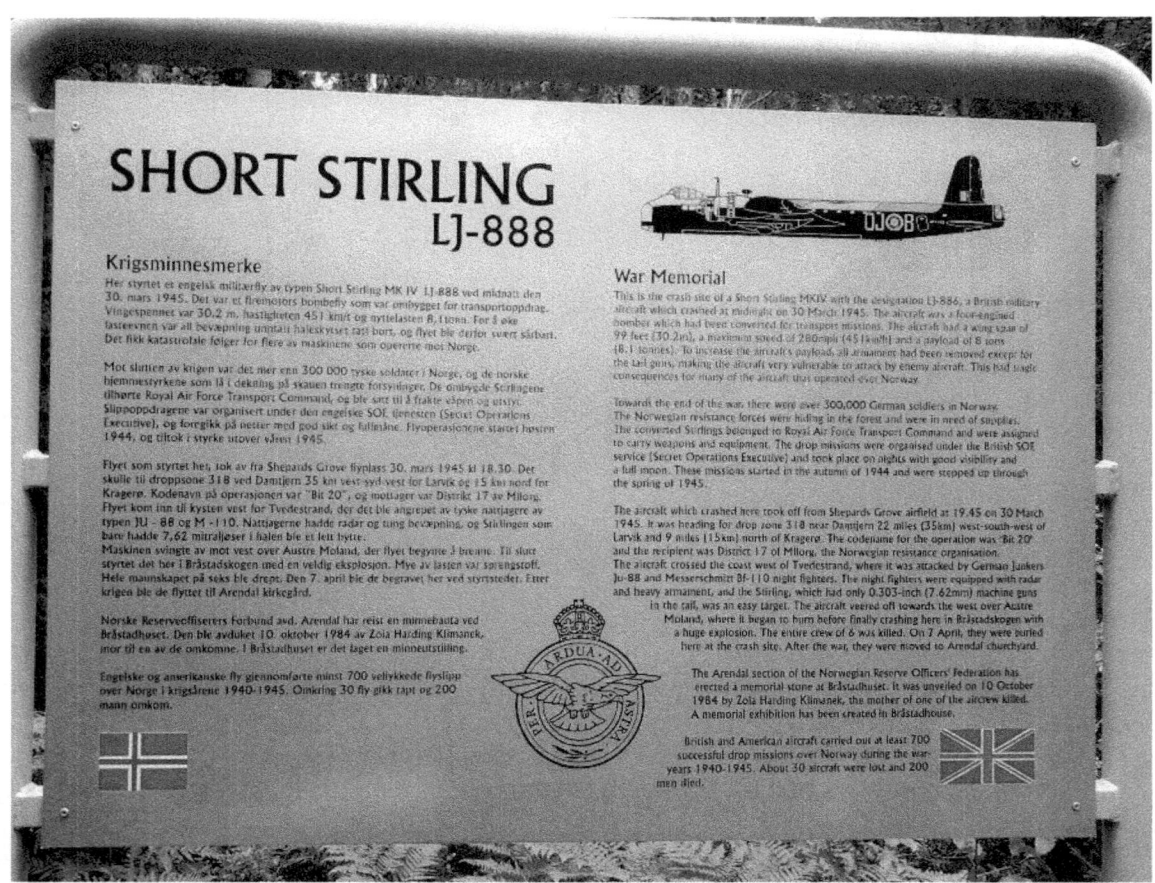

The plaque at the crash site commemorating the crew of Short Stirling LJ888.

Memorial at Brastad School, close to the crash site

Crash site.

The crew was: Pilot: P/O Clarence Campbell, Nav: F/Sgt Kenneth William Linney, A/B: F/Sgt Francis William Matthews, W/Op: W/O George Gregory Allman, F/Eng: F/Sgt Frederick Charles Brenner, A/G: F/Sgt Edward Sidney Lloyd.

It is not known what happened and the aircraft and crew was lost without trace.

W/Op: W/O George Gregory Allman

Pilot: P/O Clarence Campbell

All of the crew are commemorated on The Runnymede Memorial.

31st March: Training programme continued. No night flying programme.

This brought an end to operations for March. The squadron flew a total of 44 sorties with the loss of 12 aircrew and 3 aircraft, LJ979, LJ888 and LK197.

April 1945

1st April: Stand down weather u/s.

2nd April: Nine gliders ferried from Keevil.

Three crews briefed for operation to Norway. Two were successful.

LK193 ZO-V Piloted by P/O Carroll was missing.

The crew of LK193 was: Pilot: F/O Neville Carroll, Nav: W/O Gilbert Hughes, A/B: W/O Stanley James Verse Philo, W/Op: W/O Jack Grain, F/Eng: F/Sgt A.O. Bennett, A/G: F/Sgt Reginald Earnest Marshall.

LK193 took off at 22.30 hrs. The Stirling was heading to Norway on a S.O.E. operation codenamed 'Tablejam' carrying 24 containers and 4 panniers. The aircraft crashed off the coast of Sheringham at 22.50. Little is known of the cause of the crash that had taken place. One witness said he and his new wife were taking stroll on the beach, when they saw the Stirling heading towards the beach, he estimated that it was only a 200 ft. in altitude, then all of a sudden it exploded and crashed. Another witness said they thought one of the engines was on fire. The A.U.W. (all up weight) of the Stirling Mk.IV was 70,000lb, the AM Form 1180 (crash report) states that the 71,239lb A.U.W. of this aircraft may have been a contributing factor. It also states that the aircraft was out of control and dived in from 200ft. The aircraft was obviously in some trouble, operating above its A.U.W. could not have helped the unfortunate pilot and his young crew.

The entire crew died with the exception of F/Sgt Bennett, who later died of his injuries on June 2, 1945 and was buried at Barwell Cemetery. All the rest of the crew are buried at The Cambridge City Cemetery.

Before being transferred to 196 Squadron bomb aimer W/O Philo was in 49 Squadron flying in Lancasters. While on a bombing raid to Milan in August 1943 Lancaster LM387 which Philo was a crew member was shot down near Chartres, France. Only the navigator and Philo survived. Remarkably Philo made it to neutral Spain at the end of October after being helped by the French resistance. Unfortunately, Stanley James Verse Philo's luck finely ran out on that fateful night in April 1945.

3rd April: Beam and formation exercise carried out. Three gliders ferried from Keevil. No night flying.

W/O Stanley James Verse Philo.

F/O Neville Carroll with his wife Linda and baby son Robert, N.S.W. Australia

4th April: Bombing and glider training. One glider ferried from Fairford. Two cross countries at night.

5th April: Formation cross country carried out. Three aircraft on night map reading exercise.

6th April: Station glider exercise. Nine crews took part.

7th April: Eight crews detailed on operation to Holland, carrying containers and 15 troops each. All successful.

LK205 piloted by Maj. Rowe had damage to port tail plane caused by an S.B.C. (Small Bomb Container - canister to hold a load of the standard 4 lb. magnesium incendiary bomb - usual load was 6 to 8 SBC's).

LJ926 piloted by F/Sgt Averill had a premature fire of an S.B.C. which caused a worry to the crew.

8th April: Four crews on exercise 'Quiver' carried out, 3 successful in locating Rockall.

9th April: Limited programme due to weather.

10th April: Towing and low-level training programme. Two crews on operation to Holland. Both unsuccessful.

LK305 ZO-S piloted by F/Sgt Vernon was missing.

LK305 crew: Pilot: F/Sgt. Fredrick Vernon, Nav: W/O Kenneth Atkinson, A/B: F/O James William Whitehead, W/Op: Sgt Robert Barnes, F/Eng: Sgt. Phillip Roy Tomlinson, A/G: Sgt. Trevor Robert Jones.

LK305 for unknown reason, crashed into The Wadden Sea off the Dutch coast.

F/Sgt Vernon, Sgt Tomlinson, W/O Atkinson and Sgt Jones were never found and are remembered on The Runnymede Memorial. Sgt Jones body was found and buried in The Texel General Cemetery. F/O Whitehead's body was washed up on the 14th May at South Beach near Hoorn. He is buried in The West-Terschellin Cemetery, Netherlands.

11th April: Bombing practice carried out. Six crews on supply drop to Holland. Four were successful but two failed as no reception at D.Z.

12th April: Training programme continued. Five crews on operation to Denmark. Only one successful. Two failed due to bad weather over target.

LK362 piloted by S/Ldr Taplin was unsuccessful and reported being more or less lost and the trip was not un-exciting.

LK201 piloted by F/O Marshall was recalled due to starboard engine being u/s.

13th April: Station glider exercise, nine crews took place. Four crews detailed on operation to Norway. All crews had good successful trips.

F/O Jimmy Whitehead.

14th April: Training continued. Five crews detailed on operation to Norway. All aircraft encountered bad weather the whole trip. Four were successful, but EF309 piloted by F/Ltn Pryde didn't complete and had to land at Lossiemouth.

15th April: Training programme – low-level cross-country towing.

16th April: Training programme continued.

17th April: Nine aircraft flew to Brussels to pick up P.O.W.s and take them to R.A.F. Wescott. Each aircraft carried 27 P.O.Ws.

18th April: Ten aircraft flew to Brussels to pick up 27 P.O.W.s each. Another ten aircraft flew to Hanover with seventeen panniers of petrol each.

LK345 piloted by F/Ltn Spruell while landing in a strong crosswind on a grass strip at Hanover, the aircraft swung, and the undercarriage collapsed writing off the aircraft.

19th April: Ten aircraft flew to Hanover with panniers of petrol, then flew to Brussels to pick up P.O.Ws.

20th April: Twelve aircraft flew to Rheine to take petrol then to Brussels to pick up P.O.Ws.

21st April: Eleven aircraft flew to Rheine to take petrol then to Brussels to pick up P.O.Ws.

22nd April: Ten aircraft flew to Rheine to take petrol then to Brussels to pick up P.O.Ws.

Two aircraft detailed on operation to Denmark, only one successful.

LK368 piloted by F/O Hoystead encountered flak from many positions preventing the D.Z. to be located.

23rd April: Twelve aircraft flew to Brussels to pick up P.O.W.s to take to R.A.F Wescott, some carrying 27, some 28 and some 29 P.O.Ws.

24th April: Three aircraft on air tests otherwise the squadron was on stand down.

25th April: Six aircraft retrieved gliders from Gosfield. Five aircraft on operations, three to Norway and two to Denmark.

The three to Norway, one was successful, but two not, due to low cloud and no reception.

PW392 piloted by F/Ltn Arnold encountered an enemy aircraft but took evasive action.

The two aircraft to Denmark both encountered light flak, one was successful but one not owing to no reception.

26th April: Ten aircraft took part in a station glider exercise.

27th to 30th April: The squadron was stood down owing to bad weather.

This brought to an end, operations for April. The squadron flew a total of 114 sorties with the loss of 11 aircrew and three aircraft, LK193, LK305 and LK345.

May 1945

1st May: Twenty one crews were briefed for group glider lift exercise which was cancelled owing to adverse weather.

2nd May: Exercise again cancelled owing to the weather.

3rd May: Twenty one crews took part in the group exercise which was successful. Weather conditions prevented second lift.

4th May: Ten crews took part in group exercise, re-supply of yesterday's exercise. Very good show all round. Five crews retrieved gliders from Gosfield.

5th May: Nineteen crews went to Saltby per Group instructions. Weather not to pleasant on arrival.

The aircraft were detailed to take troops and equipment to Copenhagen.

LJ838 piloted by F/Lt Campbell had to return as the aircraft was u/s.

Pilot F/Lt Campbell RCAF and crew with ZO-N. Marked X is the rear gunner P/O George Talbot. Talbot flew many sorties on F/O McOmie's crew, which on the 20 September on a re-supply drop to Arnhem, crash landed with one of the crew being killed. He flew one more sortie with F/O Brian Arnolds crew before joining Campbell's crew.

No.196 and No.299 Squadron aircraft at Copenhagen on the 5th May 1945.

LK252 piloted by F/O Owen the aircraft was u/s.

LK312 piloted by S/Ldr Taplin the aircraft was u/s.

LJ583 piloted by F/Ltn Croft the aircraft was u/s.

LJ320 piloted by W/O Fordham the aircraft was u/s in Copenhagen.

6th May: One crew from 'A' Flight flew the odd barrel of beer to Saltby, the mess being dry from the previous night.

7th May: Fifteen crews took off from Saltby with troops for Copenhagen. Very pleasant trip. One aircraft went u/s at Copenhagen. Four aircraft returned to Saltby. One aircraft took ground crew to Copenhagen and two crews went to Brussels.

8th May: V.E. Day. Squadron given stand down from 1500 hrs to 23.59 hrs. Two crews went to Brussels.

9th May: Three crews went to Brussels.

10th May: Above crews returned.

Eight crews were detailed to Gardermoen, Norway on Operation Doomsday, taking off at 02.00 hrs. Only one crew landed owing to shocking weather, the cloud base was 400ft to 500ft with patches on the ground. All others recalled to base.

Fifteen crews took off at 07.30hrs for the same airfield, again only one crew landed due to the weather. All others recalled to base.

LK147 ZO-Z Piloted by F/O Breed crashed into high ground killing all on board, including the crew and fifteen troops.

LK147 crew was: Pilot: F/O John Leonard Breed, Nav: W/O Raymond Charles Impett, A/B: W/O Hugh Joseph Kildare, W/Op: F/Sgt David Welch, F/Eng: F/Sgt Lionel James Douglas Gilyead, A/G: F/Sgt: Harold Alfred Bell.

It is believed that Australians, Breed and Kildare were the last Aussies to be killed in 38 Group.

LK147 crashed during the approach to Gardermoen airport. The air command gave the order to return but some of the planes of that airlift did not receive the notice. LK147 was one of them. The huge bomber was seen to emerge from cloud which had a base of 200 to 300 feet. The pilot attempted an immediate climb to avoid the high ground, but the aircraft stalled, dived into the ground and burst into flames. It crashed a hundred meters from a farm. The father and son were working when they saw that it passed about thirty feet above the roof of their house. It was not on fire or smoke. It disappeared behind the treetops. There was a great explosion. As soon as they arrived at the scene of the accident, they could not do anything. Later a German detachment arrived, they had already surrendered but there were still 360,000 in the country, with a medical officer. He certified that there were no survivors. The dead were buried in a small cemetery until they were exhumed and permanently buried in Oslo in November 1945.

F/O John Leonard Breed.

W/O Hugh Joseph Kildare.

Pinpoint of crash of LK147 just short of runway. *Memorial to the crew of Stirling LK147.*

11th May: Nineteen crews were detailed to Gardermoen with troops and equipment. All had good trips.

LK256 was u/s at Gardermoen.

12th May: Nineteen crews took re-supplies for yesterday's effort. Weather was really good and all had a good trip.

Short Stirling LK357 7T-E at Stavanger 11th May 1945, with W/Op Wally Spiller and F/Eng Bill Winters.

13th May: Five crews to Gardermoen with re-supplies.

14th May: Fifteen crews detailed for Stavanger but was scrubbed.

15th May: Fifteen crews again detailed for Stavanger with 18 S.A.S. troops each. All had good trips.

16th May: Three crews detailed for Stavanger – postponed for 24 hours. Afternoon stand down until 09.00hrs on following day.

17th May: Six crews detailed to take men and supplies to Stavanger. Postponed for 24 hours.

18th May: Six crews detailed for Stavanger, left in the morning. Successful trip. All crews returned.

19th May: Seven crews detailed to bring back 6th Airborne from B.58. Take off in afternoon. To land at Chilbolton on return from B.58 and to base from there. Postponed until tomorrow.

B.58 was Melsbroek Airfield in Belgium.

20th May: Previous day's trip cancelled. Three crews detailed for Brussels. Cancelled.

21st May: Three crews detailed for B.58. Cancelled. One crew detailed for Oslo. Cancelled. Four crews detailed for Stavanger. Cancelled.

22nd May: Three crews detailed for Gardermoen and seven crews detailed for Brussels. Details for B.58 and Oslo all postponed.

23rd May: Three crews detailed for Oslo. Stayed overnight. Base unfit.

24th May: W/Cdr Turner taking spare crew to Copenhagen to collect aircraft. Three crews returned from Oslo. Squadron stand down 12.00hrs to 23.59hrs.

25th May: Four crews detailed for local towing. W/Cdr Turner and crews returned from Copenhagen.

26th May: Four crews detailed for local towing. Four crews detailed for air firing. F/Ltn Campbell taking Group Captain Troop to Carnaby.

27th May: Six crews detailed to take Canadian troops to B.58 and bring repatriated P.O.W.s to Dunsfold. Three aircraft left at Dunsfold.

28th May: One aircraft with two crews to B.58 to collect aircraft. One aircraft with two crews to Dunsfold to collect aircraft. Four crews on local flying.

29th May: Four crews on local lifts. One aircraft to Dunsfold to collect one aircraft.

30th May: Six crews to taking troops to Brussels and returning with P.O.W.s. W/Cdr Turner with Group Captain Troop to Copenhagen.

31st May: Six crews taking troops to Brussels and returning home empty. W/Cdr Turner returned from Copenhagen. One aircraft on cross country. One aircraft dumping ammo. Two crews to Dunsfold transferring P.O.W.s to Cosford and one aircraft to Dunmow taking crew to collect aircraft.

This brought to an end, operations for May. The squadron flew a total of 142 sorties with the loss of 6 aircrew and one aircraft LK147.

The crew of F/O G.R Godden RAAF are seen here with members of the 1st Border Regiment before the flight to Norway, May 15th 1945.

June 1945

1st June: Three crews detailed to B.58 taking troops and to return with repatriated troops to Dunsfold. W/O Cowan pilot of LK201 stayed overnight. One crew to Dunsfold taking spares. Two aircraft dumping ammo.

2nd June: Five crews detailed to B.58 to collect P.O.W.s and deliver to Blackbushe. Two aircraft detailed to Keevil.

3rd June: Seven aircraft detailed to take troops to B.58 and return with P.O.W.s to Blackbushe.

4th June: Five aircraft to B.58 to bring back Canadian troops to Blackbushe. One aircraft went to Tilstock.

Short Stirling 5T at Melsbroek. Note; The Hawker Typhoons of No.429 RCAF Squadron.

5th June: Five aircraft detailed to take troops to B.58 and return with Canadian troops to Blackbushe. Two aircraft on local towing.

6th June: Rain stopped play.

7th June: Weather u/s. Two aircraft did local flying for 45 mins.

8th June: One aircraft took two crews to Gt. Dunmow to bring back two new aircraft. One aircraft went to Dyce. Three crews did a bombing exercise and two did glider Cross Country.

9th June: We all went to the Derby. Stand Down.

10th June: Seven crews went to B.58 and returned to Earls Colne with Canadian troops. One crew on local flying.

11th June: Four crews on formation and one crew on local flying.

12th June: Three crews to Stavanger were cancelled. Three crews on formation flying. Six crews to B.58, five returned to Blackbushe with Canadian troops, the other back to base.

13th June: Once again Stavanger trip is cancelled. Three crews to Brussels, only one returned. Two crews on cross countries, and four crews did glider cross countries.

14th June: Crews sill standing for Stavanger. One crew returned from Brussels. Five crews carried out formation and cross country. Four crews on glider cross country in formation, and a crew went to Keevil and returned.

15th June: Ten crews took part in station glider exercise. Two crew detailed to bring back Canadian troops from Brussels to Blackbushe.

16th June: Six crews went to Stavanger and five crews went to Oslo to take troops and return with troops, all remained overnight because of bad weather. Three crews ferried aircraft to Maghaberry N.I. One crew on local towing.

17th June: One crew on cross country and three crews on formation flying. One crew took sixteen A.T.C. cadets on local cross country.

18th June: Two crews ferried aircraft to Magheberry. One crew went to Lynehem and two crews on astro cross country.

19th June: Eight crews on glider exercise, and three crews on astro cross country.

20th June: Four crews on formation flying.

21st June: One crew went to Oslo and remained as aircraft went u/s, and six crews did local towing.

22nd June: Squadron stand down.

23rd June: Six crews went to Maghaberry and two returned. Three crews did local towing and one crew did astro cross country.

24th June: Five crews went to bring gliders from Gosfield. Three crews did local towing. One crew stood by for Norway but was eventually cancelled.

25th June: Eleven crews took troops from B.58 to Dunsfold. LK128 piloted by F/Ltn Sparks, the aircraft went u/s at Dunsfold. Five crews did night astro cross country.

26th June: One crew flew spares to Oslo. One crew flew the Canadians to their repatriation centre at Snaith. One crew went to Dunsfold to bring back an aircraft

27th June: Six crews standing by for Norway. Weather u/s.

28th June: Group exercise postponed for a further 24hrs. One crew returned after spending several days at Oslo.

29th June: Six crews went to Norway, three to Oslo, and three to Stavanger, calling at East Fortune in Scotland to pick up their passengers and returning to base with troops.

30th June: Five crews took part on a station glider exercise for the benefit of some visitors. Five crews went to retrieve gliders from East Colne.

This brought an end of operations for June. The squadron flew total of 70 sorties with the loss of no aircrew or aircraft.

July 1945

1st July: One crew took some Canadians to Riccall. Three crews did cross country and one crew did an astro cross country at night.

2nd July: One crew went to East Fortune and four crews on local towing.

3rd July: Three aircraft took supplies from B.58 to Copenhagen. Four aircraft on local flying.

4th July: The three crews returned from Copenhagen. One aircraft went to East Fortune. Three crews on local towing and four crews on cross country exercise.

5th July: Weather u/s.

6th July: Squadron stand down.

7th July: Five crews detailed to take troops from Tarrant Rushton to Lubeck. One returned early with engine trouble. One aircraft went u/s at Lubeck. One aircraft went to East Fortune to collect another aircraft.

8th July: Three aircraft ferried to Maghaberry, one aircraft returned. One aircraft went to Boscombe Down. Four crews did air firing. Four aircraft on local towing.

9th July: Five crews detailed to Hamburg to pick up troops to bring back to Holmsley South. LK368 piloted by F/Lt Mather went u/s in Hamburg so returned empty. Missing aircraft returned from Lubeck via Eindhoven.

10th July: One aircraft went to Sleap Airfield and back. Ten crews briefed for group glider exercise.

11th July: Exercise postponed for 24 hours.

12th July: Exercise postponed for a further 24 hours. One aircraft went to Eindhoven to collect an aircraft. Two crews went to Ringway on attachment. One aircraft went to Leigh – on – Solent.

13th July: Ten crews took part in a group glider exercise, and later in the day retrieved the gliders from Rivenhall. Thirteen crews were briefed for Norway.

14th July: Norway trip cancelled. Remaining aircraft returned from Hamburg.

15th July: Twelve crews took off to pick up troops at East Fortune, then on to Oslo.

16th July: Crews returned from Oslo. Four aircraft diverted to Leuchars, one to Carnaby and one to Boulmer, the remainder with one exception (who remained in Oslo) returned with troops to East Fortune.

17th July: One crew went to Oslo. Some aircraft on local flying and two crews did night astro cross country.

18th July: Six crews on formation cross country, four crews did local towing and two crews on night astro cross country.

19th July: The last aircraft returned from Oslo via East Fortune. Six aircraft did formation flying and four aircraft did local towing.

20th July: Squadron stand down.

21st July: One aircraft did cross country training. Four aircraft did local towing, and two aircraft did glider cross country.

22nd July: Two aircraft on training cross country. Two aircraft did fighter affiliation and low flying, and four aircraft did local towing. At night three crews did astro cross-country.

23rd July: Three crews did local flying.

24th July: Ten crews got away on a group glider exercise. Later in the day, crews went to Rivenhall to retrieve eight gliders.

25th July: Nine crews detailed to take troops to Oslo. Two of the aircraft, LJ876 and LK320 were u/s at Oslo. Four crews did local towing.

26th July: Three aircraft ferried displaced persons from Brussels to Copenhagen. Three aircraft ferried A.T.S. from Brussels to Schleswig-Holstein. Two aircraft ferried R.A.F. Personnel from Copenhagen to Horham, the third aircraft being u/s at Copenhagen. One aircraft to Oslo. Four aircraft on local towing.

27th July: One aircraft did local towing.

28th July: One aircraft to Schleswig-Holstein, also four aircraft on towing as well as two aircraft on local towing.

29th July: Training programme, four aircraft on towing, one aircraft on fighter affiliation and one aircraft did a training cross country.

30th July: Four aircraft on towing, and one aircraft on local flying at night. Four aircraft on Astro Cross Country.

31st July: One aircraft went to Copenhagen. Four aircraft on local towing and two aircraft on local flying. Two aircraft on astro cross country.

This brought to an end, operations for July. The squadron flew a total of 36 sorties with no loss of aircrew or aircraft.

August 1945

1st August: Twelve aircraft helped to move equipment and personnel of 1665 H.C.U. from Saltby to Marston Moor.

2nd August: Ten aircraft were detailed to take R.C.A.F. personnel and kit from Warmwell to B164 (Schleswig-Holstein) and returned to Warmwell with similar load. One aircraft returned to base from Warmwell with no load.

3rd August: Stand down.

4th August: No flying owing to internal move of living quarters.

5th August: One aircraft to Oslo. One aircraft filming.

6th August: No flying.

7th August: Training programme. Local flying and towing.

8th August: Ten aircraft detailed for Prague, and subsequently postponed 24 hours. Local towing and mass take off. Five aircraft for film unit.

9th August: Weather poor. Three aircraft on local towing. One aircraft to Pershore and return. One aircraft local flying for film.

10th August: Three aircraft on formation and one aircraft on local flying.

11th August: One aircraft did a container trip.

12th August: No flying.

13th August: Nine aircraft went to Prague carrying displaced personnel and returned to Crosby with children. One aircraft went u/s at Crosby, the rest returned to base.

One aircraft and crew who undertook the repatriation of P.O.W.s and replacement of orphans was LK368 ZO-Q.

The crew of LK368 was: Pilot: P/O E.A. Turner, A.B: F/Sgt G.S. Lashbrook, F/Eng: Sgt R.G. Cotton, Nav: F/O O.K.D. Busby, W/Op: F/Sgt J.F. Lunt, A/G: P.C. Kite.

These are the recollections of W/Op Jack Lunt:

"On one occasion, the crew were dropping paratroopers. This time, they were dropping through the bottom of the plane behind enemy lines. I had to climb down into the bottom of the plane which was shaped like a large bath tub. I then had to undo 2 wing-nuts at one end. The tub then lifted in the air with the updraft, and I secured the wing-nuts in that position. Next I had to walk back along a ledge of 4 to 6 inches to his seat. One of the paratroopers said, 'I wouldn't want your job', but I was thinking, I wouldn't want your job dropping behind enemy lines.

On another occasion when dropping paratroopers, Lunt said that their rank did not count in the air. On one occasion, it was their sergeant in charge, as he was the strongest and most frightening. His job was to kick the paratroopers out of the plane. Their parachutes were attached to a cable which deployed the parachute as the left the aircraft. The sergeant was to make sure no-one hesitated, or else their landings would be miles apart. The commanding officer warned the sergeant not to kick him too hard, as on the ground he would be of lower rank, and would suffer the consequences.

During a few missions, probably S.O.E., Jack spoke about dropping a man in Norway. He was to get to Oslo and gather intelligence on German operations there, then return to Britain. The unusual thing was that the same crew would be dropping him again a few weeks later. This had the crew baffled, as he would not have gained much in such a short time.

It wasn't until the end of the war that they found out they had been dropping twins. One would replace the other, whilst the other would return with the gathered intelligence.

On another mission, Jack's crew dropped a spy on a mountain in Scandinavia, possibly Sweden. What was unusual was that she was a female, 81 years old, in full all white skiing gear.

When recovering orphans and P.O.W.s from the camps, Jack spoke of how quiet it was. The strange thing was that there was no bird song, something that we take for granted.

As Jack Lunt was from Liverpool, he was not always able to get home when he had a pass. Passes varied and could be 24 hours or 48 hours. On one occasion he was travelling home, but on arrival at Lime Street station in Liverpool, he was met by Military Police. They gave him another ticket to re-board a train and go to Scotland. When he arrived there, the same thing happened, and he was given a ticket to somewhere else in England. He ended up spending his weekend leave travelling around Britain on trains. When he got back to camp, they explained that it was to confuse German intelligence into thinking that there were mass movement of troops.

On one weekend pass, Jack travelled to Somerset to the home of his mate and fellow crew member, Kite. At dinner, Kite's mother was pouring glasses of cider for the family (children included) and asked Jack what he would like to drink.

Not wishing to be rude, he said cider would be fine. After dinner, he and Kite went out for the night, where they partook of a few more ciders. Lunt said he had never had a hangover as bad as that night. Unfortunately, he woke early in the morning and had a drink of water before Kite's family could stop him. He said it made him as drunk as the night before.

Crew of Short Stirling LK368

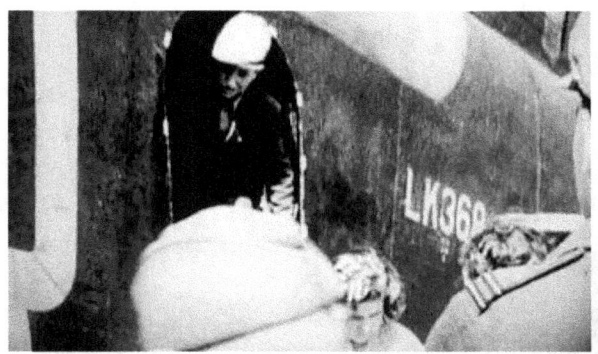

Repatriation of P.O.W.s and orphans by LK368

Jack Lunt was a pianist and would play the piano in the mess. They would normally sing songs like, The Quartermaster's Stores, or anything else to lift their spirits. However, one member of the squadron was called Akis Kumas, so Jack would play the memorable song from Casablanca, As Time Goes By. Everyone would join in to sing, Kumas remember this, a kiss is just Akis.

14th August: One aircraft to Prague and return to Crosby.

15th August: No flying, V.J. Day.

16th August: No flying, V.J. Day +1

17th August: Four aircraft on formation and two aircraft on cross country.

LK368 with skipper P/O E.A. Turner seated.

W/Op F/Sgt John (Jack) Lunt.

A time to reflect, Short Stirling Mk.IV LK368 ZO-Q at dispersal.

18th August: One aircraft did an air test. Seven crews briefed for Copenhagen. Four crews briefed for Schleswig-Holstein and five crews for Prague.

19th August: Five aircraft went to Copenhagen via Warmwell. Two aircraft returned to base from Warmwell. Four aircraft went to Schleswig-Holstein via Warmwell and all returned to Base. Four aircraft went to Manston to pick up their load for Prague.

20th August: All aircraft returned from Copenhagen. Six crews briefed for Prague.

21st August: Prague trip postponed. One aircraft returned from Prague. Two aircraft on local flying.

22nd August: Three aircraft on flying with film unit. Prague trip postponed. Two aircraft returned from Prague via Berlin and Stoney Cross.

23rd August: One aircraft went to Marston Moor. Five aircraft on flying for film purposes.

24th August: Six aircraft to Prague with freight and troops. One aircraft to Berlin. All other flying cancelled.

25th August: Two aircraft returned from Berlin and six aircraft returned from Prague.

26th August: Three aircraft flying for film purposes. The film production which the squadron's aircraft were being used for was a French production in conjunction with Pathe called Bataillon Du Ciel, about French paratroopers.

27th August: Eight aircraft went to Prague with freight and troops. Five aircraft on paratroop dropping for the film. One aircraft took freight to Stoney Cross.

28th August: One aircraft to Blackbushe and one aircraft to Pershore.

29th and 30th August: No flying.

31st August: One aircraft to Marston Moor and one aircraft to Stoney Cross. Four aircraft on glider cross country. Two aircraft on night astro cross country.

This brought to an end, operations for August. The squadron flew a total of 59 sorties with no loss of aircrew or aircraft.

The following photographs are stills from the film 'Le Bataillon Du Ciel' and depict Stirlings of No.196 Squadron.

September 1945

1st September: One aircraft to Church Lawford and return. Three aircraft on local towing. One aircraft on local flying and one aircraft on air test.

2nd September: Station stand down, 'B' Flight on standby.

3rd September: Nine aircraft on glider exercise. One aircraft on filming. One aircraft on range flying and one aircraft on local flying.

4th September: Standing by for group glider exercise, which was postponed for 24 hours. One aircraft on air test.

5th September: Five aircraft went to Portreath for freight then on to Karachi, India. Group glider exercise again postponed for 24 hours. One aircraft on air test.

6th September: Ten aircraft on group glider exercise. 110 containers dropped on aerodrome.

7th September: One aircraft on range flying, and to Portreath and return. One aircraft on air test. Four aircraft on night cross country.

8th September: One aircraft to Marston Moor. One aircraft over France with film unit.

9th September: Stand down.

10th September: One aircraft to Pershore. Two aircraft to Bordeaux, one aircraft was replacement for aircraft on India run.

11th September: Two aircraft to Marseille, one aircraft was replacement aircraft on India run.

12th September: One aircraft returned from Bordeaux with two crews, and one aircraft returned from Marseille with two crews.

13th September: Ten aircraft on station glider exercise, recalled after 20 minutes, weather u/s. One aircraft on local flying for film unit.

14th September: Three aircraft on air firing, only one completed exercise.

15th September: One aircraft to Methwold and one aircraft to Llanbedr both with gliders. Two aircraft on local flying. One aircraft returned from Mildenhall.

16th September: One aircraft took another crew to Prague to bring back another aircraft. One aircraft returned from Foulsham. One aircraft on local flying.

17th September: One aircraft did low flying over Normandy for film unit. One aircraft returned from Llanbedr. One aircraft took a spare crew to Stoney Cross to collect aircraft. Both returned.

18th September: Nine crews briefed foe group glider exercise.

19th September: Group exercise postponed for 24 hours. Two aircraft did local flying. One aircraft returned from India.

20th September: Group exercise postponed for another 24 hours.

21st September: Ten aircraft took place in a group glider exercise.

22nd September: Two aircraft ferried to Stoney Cross. Two aircraft on local flying.

23rd September: No flying.

24th September: Second aircraft returned from India with crew of u/s aircraft.

25th September: No flying.

26th September: Third aircraft returned from India.

27th September: One aircraft to Brize Norton and return.

28th September: Fourth and last aircraft returned from India. Three aircraft did air tests.

29th September: One aircraft to Melton Mowbray.

30th September: No flying.

This brought to an end, operations for September. The squadron flew a total of 12 sorties with no loss of aircrew and 1 aircraft lost. The aircraft was LK326 which burst a tyre on take-off and belly landed, in India, writing it off.

October 1945

1st October: One aircraft returned from Melton Mowbray.

2nd October: One aircraft took spares to Toulouse. One aircraft picked supplies up at Stoney Cross then took them to Karachi, India. One aircraft took a crew to Brussels to collect an aircraft. Ten crews briefed for group exercise.

3rd October: Ten aircraft took part in a group exercise. One aircraft did a night astro exercise. One aircraft returned from Toulouse.

4th October: Three aircraft detailed to Brussels to pick up troops then on to Cairo West and return with troops. Two aircraft to Earls Colne with spare crew to pick up a u/s aircraft and retrieve gliders.

5th October: One aircraft to Cairo West to pick up troops and return to base. One aircraft from Earls Colne and one aircraft to Matching and return.

Keith Franklin of F/Lt C.A. Swaddling's crew in front of ZO-W which was used to ferry troops to Cairo.

6th October: No flying.

7th October: Three aircraft on air tests.

8th October: Three aircraft to Brussels to pick up troops and on to Cairo West. One aircraft on air test.

9th October: One aircraft to Istres, France. Two aircraft to Brussels for troops and on to Cairo West.

F/Eng Keith Franklin at Shepherds Grove, October 1945.

10th October: One aircraft to Cairo and one aircraft to Holme to pick troops up and on to Qastina, Palastine.

11th October: Two aircraft to Cairo via Brussels. One aircraft on air test.

12th October: One aircraft to Brussels then to Cairo West. One aircraft to Holme then on to Palestine.

13th October: One aircraft to Brussels and on to Cairo West.

14th October: No flying.

15th October: Two aircraft on local flying.

16th October: Four aircraft on local flying.

17th October: One aircraft to Istres and return. One aircraft to B.77 and return. Three aircraft on local flying.

18th October: Three aircraft did container dropping. One aircraft returned from Cairo.

19th October: Two aircraft to Brussels then to Cairo West. Two other aircraft returned from Cairo. Two aircraft on night cross country and two on local flying.

20th October: Two aircraft to Brussels then Cairo West.

21st October: Two aircraft to Brussels then Cairo West.

22nd October: One aircraft to Brussels then Cairo West. One aircraft to Istres and one aircraft on air test.

23rd October: One aircraft to Cairo West.

24th October: One aircraft to Cairo but returned after 20 minutes flying. One aircraft returned from Cairo.

25th October: One aircraft to Oakington for troops to Cairo West.

26th October: No flying.

27th October: Two aircraft to Oakington then Cairo West. One aircraft took a crew to pick up an aircraft at Istres. Three aircraft returned from Cairo.

28th October: One to Oakington then Cairo West.

29th October: No flying.

30th October: One aircraft on local flying.

31st October: One aircraft on local towing.

This brought an end to operations for October. The squadron flew a total of 30 sorties with no loss of aircrew or aircraft.

November 1945

1st November: One aircraft on local flying.

2nd November: Two aircraft on local flying.

3rd November: One aircraft to Prestwick and return. One aircraft on air test. Four aircraft returned from Cairo.

4th November: Three aircraft detailed to take freight from Aldergrove to Church Broughton.

5th November: One aircraft returned from Cairo.

6th November: Two aircraft on local flying.

7th November: Ten aircraft on glider exercise. Three aircraft returned from Aldergrove.

8th November: Three aircraft detailed to take freight from Aldergrove to Church Broughton. Six aircraft ferried gliders to Sealand.

9th November: Two aircraft returned from Aldergrove.

10th November: One aircraft detailed to Orly to take freight to Copenhagen.

11th November: One aircraft to Rivenhall.

12th November: One aircraft and another crew to collect an aircraft from Bordeaux.

13th November: One aircraft on local towing.

14th November: One aircraft detailed to take freight to Cairo West and one aircraft to pick up freight at Lyneham to take to Luga, Russia. Five aircraft did astro cross country at night.

15th November: Check Parade. No flying.

16th November: One aircraft to Lossiemouth. One aircraft on local flying and one on local towing.

17th, 18th and 19th November: No flying.

20th November: No flying. Preparation for A.O.C.s visit – check parade.

21st November: No flying.

22nd November: A.O.C.s Parade.

23rd November: Two aircraft on local flying. One aircraft retrieved a glider. Cross country – Lossiemouth.

24th November: One aircraft on local flying.

25th November: Two aircraft on local towing and one aircraft on local flying.

26th November: Detailed to pick freight up at Lyneham and take to Almasa (Cairo). Five aircraft on local towing.

27th November: Seven aircraft on local towing and one on astro cross country.

28th November: Three aircraft on local towing. One aircraft to Netheravon and back with freight.

29th November: Eight aircraft on local towing. One aircraft to B.58.

30th November: One aircraft with two crews to Aldergrove to collect another aircraft. Two aircraft on local towing.

This brought to an end, operations for November. The squadron flew a total of 12 sorties with the loss of no aircrew or aircraft.

December 1945

1st December: Local towing and flying.

2nd December: No flying.

3rd December: Local towing.

4th December: One aircraft to Lyon to pick up a now serviceable aircraft.

5th December: Ten aircraft on group glider exercise. One aircraft on local flying.

6th December: No day flying. Four aircraft on night cross countries.

7th and 8th December: No flying.

9th December: Local flying.

10th and 11th December: No flying due to weather.

12th December: One aircraft on test of 'G' airfield approach at Gt. Dunmow.

13th December: Two aircraft on local towing. One aircraft to Gt. Dunmow. One aircraft to Wethersfield.

14th December: Seven gliders dispersed from Gosfield to Cosford.

15th to 18th December: No flying due to weather.

19th December: Two aircraft on air tests. Two aircraft on local towing.

20th December: Eight aircraft on glider exercise, 'Stockyard'.

21st December: One aircraft on cross country.

23rd to 26th December: Xmas Grant.

27th December: One aircraft to Ouston and return.

28th and 29th December: No flying.

30th December: Five aircraft on local towing.

31st December: No flying.

This brought to an end, operations for December.

The squadron flew no sorties this month.

January 1946

1st January: Two aircraft on local towing.

2nd January: Ten aircraft carried out glider dispersal from Gosfield to Cosford.

3rd January: Eleven aircraft carried out glider dispersal from Cosford to Brize Norton.

4th January: One aircraft was detailed to collect a Halifax main wheel from Tarrant Rushton to Bordeaux and returned with u/s wheel. Two aircraft on local towing and two on local flying.

5th January: No flying.

6th January: Two aircraft on local towing.

7th January: One aircraft on local towing.

8th January: W/Cdr J. Blackburn D.S.O. - D.F.C. assumed command of the squadron. W/Cdr R.T.F. Turner D.F.C. about to be released under Class "A" Release.

Arrival of nineteen crews and twelve selected aircraft (Stirling Mk IV) from No. 570 Squadron, Rivenhall, which was disbanded with effect from today. The intention was to supplement the strength of 196 Squadron to 36 crews. Nineteen crews were selected from 570 Squadron and seventeen from 196 Squadron. The redundant crews from each squadron being posted elsewhere. S/Ldr Bullen assumed command of 'B' Flight which comprised of 18 crews from 570 Squadron, and S/Ldr Pryde in command of 'A' Flight with 17 crews from 196 Squadron and 1 crew from 570 Squadron.

9th January: Six aircraft were detailed to collect ground crews from Rivenhall.

10th January: Four aircraft carried out local flying. One aircraft was detailed to collect ground crews from Rivenhall. One aircraft was engaged on night flying practice at Valley.

11th January: One aircraft collected ground staff from Rivenhall.

12th January: Four crews flew to Rivenhall to collect equipment and remaining ground staff. One aircraft flew to Tarrant Rushton. Three crews carried out a six-hour night cross country navigational exercise.

13th January: One aircraft on local flying. Four crews carried out Gee approach landings on base and G.C.A. practice at Manston.

14th January: Two aircraft on local flying. One crew practiced Gee approach landings on base. Three crews were detailed to do a six-hour night cross country navigational exercise. One aircraft went u/s after being airborne 15 minutes. One aircraft flew to St. Mawgan to collect a sand blower.

15th January: The squadron was today allotted the task of mail delivery to the continent in conjunction with 299 Squadron. Each squadron to be engaged on the scheduled mail runs on alternate days. 196 Squadron commenced this duty today.

General information in connection with scheduled mail and newspaper service to the Continent.

This service has been in operation since the 5th September 1945 with Stirlings from Rivenhall. With effect from the 15th January 1946 the service will be operated by Stirlings from Shepherds Grove, Suffolk.

Intention, to operate a scheduled newspaper and mail service between the United Kingdom and the Continent primarily for the benefit of British occupation forces.

Seven aircraft successfully completed the mail runs, but W/O Crane in 7T-E, could not land at Schleswig on account of fog, and was diverted to 104 Staging Post, Hamburg, where he was detained with engine trouble. Two crews on local flying.

16th January: Seven aircraft successfully completed the scheduled mail runs to the Continent. The squadron continued to carry out all transport tasks until 299 Squadron was sufficiently re-organised to take over on alternate days.

Three aircraft flew to Rivenhall to collect ground staff posted to the station. Three crews on local flying and one crew carried out a cross country navigational exercise.

17th January: Seven aircraft on mail delivery to the Continent. Six aircraft returned but W/O Hunt in LK128 7T-M was detained in Schleswig with engine trouble.

One crew in a Mk V Stirling collected a Halifax main wheel at Earls Court and delivered to Boscombe Down. Two crews on 4 hour cross country training flight.

18th January: Seven aircraft successfully delivered mail to the Continent.

19th January: 'B' Flight personnel had a stand down over the weekend (18th to 20th).

Seven aircraft on mail delivery.

20th January: All flying cancelled due to fog bound conditions at the base.

21st January: Flying cancelled again due to fog.

22nd January: Six aircraft to the Continent on mail run. Three aircraft on local flying.

W/O Hunt and crew returned from Schleswig in LK199, his own aircraft still u/s there since the 17th January.

23rd January: Seven aircraft to the Continent on mail run.

LJ926 ZO-K piloted by F/Ltn Mather was u/s at Schleswig.

LK205 ZO-D piloted by W/O Baron was u/s at Schleswig.

Short Stirling LK205 ZO-D on troop deploying after V.E.-Day. Note; German soldier in front of the truck.

Three crews practiced ground control approach landings at Tibenham airfield and Gee approach landings at base.

Three crews on cross country and three crews on night circuits and landings.

24th January: Four crews practiced standard beam approach landings – two at Woodbridge and two at Earls Colne.

25th January: Seven aircraft on mail run. LK362 7T-R piloted by W/O Marshall was u/s at Handorf.

26th January: All flying was cancelled due to cloud base at ground level.

27th January: W/O Baron returned from Schleswig and W/O Marshall returned from Handorf.

Seven aircraft on mail run. LK117 7T-B piloted by W/Cdr Blackburn had to make an emergency landing at Woodbridge because of low brake pressure. They returned to base by road.

28th January: Three crews were flown to collect 3 Mk V Stirlings allotted to the squadron (Nos. PJ912, PK128 and PJ986).

F/Lt Shuter collected 7T-B from Woodbridge.

29th January: Seven aircraft on mail run.

30ᵗʰ January: Two crews ferried two Stirlings Mk IV (LK201 and LK242) which were surplus to requirements to No. 23 M.U. Maghaberry, N. Ireland. F/Ltn Boyd flew the two crews back to base.

Three crews collected the following MkV Stirlings from Stradishall which were allotted to the squadron, PJ974, PK126 and PK127. F/Lt Downing flew the crews to Stradishall.

31ˢᵗ January: 'B' Flight continued to carry out the mail runs while 'A' Flight personnel wrote examinations for the purpose of re-categorising aircrew.

Seven aircraft carried out the mail run. One crew ferried Stirling Mk V PJ981 from Wratting Common.

This brought to an end, operations for January. The squadron flew a total of 73 sorties with no loss of aircrew or aircraft.

A Stirling Mk IV receives attention from engineering staff at the technical site at Keevil.

February 1946

Unfortunately, it appears that the Operation Records Books for the month of February 1946 at The National Archives are missing. Therefore, it is impossible to relate what actually occurred for this month. There is one thing though, it is known that the squadron did carry on doing the Continental mail runs. Probably the rest of the month was just the mundane training that the crews seem to do most days.

Two photos taken in Feb/Mar 1946 at Rivenhall of PK144 in its natural metal finish.

March 1946

1st March: Seven aircraft were detailed for the Continental mail runs. Six were successful, but PK885 7T-V piloted by W/O Fordham, on the Brussels Run, had encountered poor weather conditions and had to return to base with their load.

2nd March: Poor weather conditions with heavy snowstorms caused all transport tasks to be cancelled.

3rd March: Snowstorms still prevailed. Eight crews successfully completed the mail runs. The following crews returned from the Continent, where they were detained through engine trouble, F/Ltn Lawson, F/Ltn Torrens, W/O Barron and W/O Beveridge.

4th March: Weather was still poor with low cloud and rain. Seven crews took off on the mail runs and stayed overnight on the Continent on account of poor weather conditions at base.

5th March: Still adverse weather conditions with low cloud and drizzle.

Seven crews detailed on the mail runs, five returned.

PJ974 piloted by F/O Kean's aircraft was u/s at Handorf with a broken tail wheel, broken towing end ring and S/I Magneto trouble.

PJ887 piloted by F/Ltn Mather's aircraft was u/s at Buckenburg with a u/s w/t.

6th March: Weather again poor with low cloud. Seven aircraft took off on the mail runs. Two crews returned to base, but the other five stayed overnight at various staging posts on the Continent.

The following Stirling Mk IVs PW449 7T-K and PW420 ZO-J which had come surplus to requirements were ferried to No. 23 M.U., N. Ireland. F/Lt Jones flew the crews back to base.

7th March: Seven crews successfully completed the mail runs.

S/Ldr Bullen collected 7T-F from Brussels where it was u/s.

W/O Barron collected 5G-J from Buckenburg where it was u/s.

F/Sgt Peacock collected ZO-O from Buckenburg where it was u/s.

LK289 ZO-M piloted by F/O Wright flew the aircraft to No. 23 M.U. as surplus.

Three photos of Peter Richens. Left: Seen here while training. Centre : Home on leave with his flying gear. Right : A qualified Flight Engineer.

8th March: Six aircraft successfully completed the mail runs.

Mail run BBA (Brussels) was cancelled for Stirlings as from today, and Anson crews from the Continent were temporarily attached to the station to carry out this task.

Four Dakota crews arrived from Membury to fly as supernumerary crews on the mail runs to gain experience.

F/Sgt Peacock and crew with F/Sgt Richens top left.   *F/Sgt Peter Richens with his mother and father.*

9th March: Six crews successfully completed the mail runs.

10th March: Six crews successfully completed the mail runs.

11th March: Mail schedule to Handorf was cancelled with effect today.

Five aircraft completed the mail runs.

The following Stirlings, PJ986, LK250 and LK303 had become surplus to requirements and were ferried to No, 23 M.U. in N. Ireland. W/O Loxham in 7T-V flew the crews back to base.

12th March: Five aircraft completed the mail runs.

13th March: Five crews took off on the mail runs, but stayed overnight on the Continent, due to the bad weather at Base.

14th March: Five crews completed the mail runs.

The five crews returned to base from the previous day.

W/Cdr Blackburn collected LK559 V8-Q from Schleswig, where it had been u/s for some time.

F/Lt Boyd and W/O Eyles collected two aircraft that had been u/s at Brussels.

15th March: Five aircraft took off on the mail runs. PJ955 ZO-U piloted by F/Sgt Davies was detained at Schleswig with engine trouble.

As from today all mail transport tasks will be carried out by R.A.F. Station Membury in Dakotas and No.196 Squadron commences to be disbanded.

All Stirling aircraft to be disposed of at No. 23 Maintenance Unit (Maghaberry and Aldergrove, N. Ireland).

16th March: P/O Jeffries flew F/Sgt Peacock and crew to Buckenburg to collect ZO-O which had been u/s there. W/O Averill flew W/O Beveridge and crew to Schleswig to collect V8-C which had been u/s there since November '45.

17th March: Two crews were engaged on local flying giving A.T.C. cadets flying experience.

18th March: The following aircraft were ferried to No. 23 M.U. for disposal. LK341, LK301, LK232, LK554 and PW415.

19th March: F/Sgt Davies in X9-P flew the crews from No. 23 M.U. back to base.

A squadron photograph of all aircrew was taken today.

20th March: W/O Beveridge collected and returned in V8-C from Schleswig.

21st March: F/Sgt Peacock collected and returned PJ974 from Buckeburg where it had been u/s since the 5th.

F/Lt Murphy flew to Schleswig to collect ground crew and repair equipment.

The following aircraft were flown to No. 23 M.U. for disposal, LK643, PK126 and LJ879. F/Lt Boyd flew the crews back to base.

22nd March: The following Stirlings were ferried to No 23 M.U. for disposal, PW461, LJ821 and EF275. F/Lt Murphy flew the crews back to base.

Aircrew personnel as detailed in Appendix 175 were cleared and proceeded on a weekend pass prior to being posted to R.A.F. Stations Pocklington and Snaith.

23rd March: No flying.

24th March: The disbandment of No. 196 Squadron was completed today.

All remaining squadron personnel were posted to Station Headquarters, R.A.F. Station Shepherd Grove with effect from 25/3/46.

The disposal of the remaining Stirling aircraft on the station will be attended to by station operations.

This brought to an end, operations for March and the squadron. The squadron flew a total of 86 Sorties with no loss of aircrew or aircraft.

196 Squadron in front of a Stirling Mk.V at RAF Rivenhall March 1946 just before the disbandment of the squadron.

Appendix I: Aircraft

Vickers Wellington Mk X

There was 11,461 Wellingtons built between 1936 and 1945, there were 22 variants from the Mk I to the T Mk XIX. The squadron was mainly equipped with the Mk X from January 1943 until July 1943. The Mk X was the last version of the Wellington to be designed as a strategic bomber. It was similar to the Mk III, but used the Hercules VI or XVII engine, providing 1,675 hp. The weight of the fuselage was reduced by the use of new light alloys in place of the steel used in earlier versions. The Mk X had a longer range than the Mk III, but a smaller bomb load, although at 4,000lbs this was still enough to carry the 'blockbuster' bomb. The Mk X had a very short career as a front line bomber with Bomber Command in Britain, it first entered service in late 1942, equipped twelve squadrons by March 1943, and had been entirely replaced by the new four engine heavies by the end of 1943. It remained in use as a bomber in Italy and the Far East throughout 1944. In all 3,803 Mk Xs were produced, and some remained in use until the 1950s. The Mk X flew its last Bomber Command mission in October 1943, at the time as the Mk III. The Wellington was nicknamed the Wimpy by RAF personnel, after the portly J. Wellington Wimpy character from the Popeye cartoons.

General characteristics:

Crew: five or six. Length: 64 ft 7 in (19.69 m) Wingspan: 86 ft 2 in (26.26 m) Height: 17 ft 5 in (5.31 m) Wing area: 840 sq ft (78 m2) Empty weight: 18,556 lb (8,417 kg). Maximum take-off weight: 28,500 lb (12,927 kg)

Powerplant: 2 × Bristol Pegasus Mark XVII radial engines, 1,050 hp (780 kW) each

Performance:

Maximum speed: 235 mph (378 km/h, 204 km) at 15,500 ft (4,700 m) Range: 2,550 mi (4,100 km, 2,220 nmi) Service ceiling: 18,000 ft (5,500 m) Rate of climb: 1,120 ft/min (5.7 m/s)

Armament Guns: 4–8× .303 Browning machine guns: 2× in nose turret, 2× in tail turret. Bombs: 4,500 lb (2,000 kg) bombs.

The squadron lost a total of 21 Wellingtons while in service. The serial numbers were:

SERIAL	FAILED TO RETURN
HE162	May 1943
HE165	February 1943
HE166	April 1943
HE167	March 1943
HE167	March 1943
HE168	April 1943
HE169	February 1943
HE170	April 1943
HE171	July 1943
HE181	March 1943
HE220	April 1943
HE385	March 1943
HE387	April 1943
HE395	April 1943
HE398	May 1943
HE412	June 1943
HE469	April 1943
HE548	March 1943
HE980	July 1943
HZ478	July 1943
MS491	June 1943

Short Stirling Mks III, IV and V

There was 2,383 Short Stirlings built between 1939 and 1946, although it was 1941 before it became operational. The Stirling was the first four engined bomber. There were several variant from the Mk I to The Mk V. The squadron used the Mk III for bombing when it replaced the Wellingtons in August 1943. It was eventually taken off mainstream bombing after heavy losses. The squadron left Bomber Command in November 1943 and the Stirling was then equipped with the Mk IV (pictured) which was converted as a glider tug and troop transporter. Some Mk Vs was used not long before the squadron was disbanded in March 1946.

General characteristics:

Crew: 6 or 7. Length: 87 ft 3 in (26.59 m), Wingspan: 99 ft 1 in (30.20 m), Height: 22 ft 9 in (6.93 m), Wing area: 1,460 sq ft (136 m2), Empty weight: 49,600 lb (22,498 kg), Gross weight: 59,400 lb (26,943 kg), Max take-off weight: 70,000 lb (31,751 kg)

Powerplant: 4 × Bristol Hercules XI 14-cylinder air-cooled sleeve-valve radial piston engines, 1,500 hp (1,100 kW) each

Propellers: 3-bladed metal fully feathering constant-speed propeller, 13 ft 6 in (4.11 m) diameter

Performance:

Maximum speed: 282 mph (454 km/h) at 12,500 ft (3,800 m), Cruise speed: 200 mph (320 km/h).

Range: 2,330 mi (3,750 km)

Service ceiling: 16,500 ft (5,000 m).

Rate of climb: 800 ft/min (4.1 m/s).

Armament:

Guns: 8 x 0.303 in (7.7 mm) Browning machine guns: 2 in powered nose turret, 4 in tail turret, 2 in dorsal turret.

Bombs: Up to 14,000 lb (6,350 kg) of bombs.

Although around 160 Stirlings were allotted to the squadron some were transferred to other squadrons if damaged and repaired. Most were S.O.C. (struck of charge) at the disbandment of the squadron.

The squadron lost a total of 44 Stirlings while in service. The serial numbers were:

SERIAL	FAILED TO RETURN
BK663	September 1943
BK771	February 1944
EE964	September 1943
EE973	September 1943
EF114	September 1943
EF234	November 1944
EF248	September 1944
EF311	August 1944
EF464	October 1943
EF468	February 1944
EF469	February 1944
EF494	October 1943
EH952	August 1943
EH960	October 1943
EH961	August 1943
EJ110	February 1944
LJ564	July 1944
LJ810	September 1944
LJ834	March 1944
LJ839	March 1944
LJ840	September 1944
LJ841	June 1944
LJ842	April 1944
LJ843	September 1944
LJ851	September 1944
LJ870	February 1945
LJ888	March 1945
LJ894	February 1945
LJ925	February 1945
LJ928	September 1944
LJ947	September 1944
LJ949	September 1944
LJ954	September 1944
LJ979	March 1945
LJ988	September 1944
LK126	February 1945
LK142	September 1944

LK147	May 1945
LK193	April 1945
LK197	March 1945
LK305	April 1945
LK326	September 1945
LK345	April 1945
LK556	September 1944

Appendix II: Sorties

The squadron, from its first sortie in early 1943, until it disbanded in March 1946 flew a total of 2,127 sorties. These have been broken down in to three sections. The first when in Bomber Command from November 1942 until October 1943, secondly when in No.38 Group, Allied Expeditionary Air Force (AEAF) from November 1943 until May 1945, and thirdly although still in 38 Group the sorties are for when the war and hostilities had ceased from June 1945 till the disbandment of the squadron in March 1946.

Also the chop rates (losses) are obtained by an elementary calculation of relating monthly sorties to aircraft losses.

DATE	SORTIES	AIRCREW LOST	AIRCRAFT LOST
January 1943	11	2	0
February 1943	113	10	2
March 1943	97	14	4
April 1943	103	30	8
May 1943	109	10	2
June 1943	123	6	3
July 1943	53	11	3
Totals	609	83	22

Chop rate: 3.61%

DATE	SORTIES	AIRCREW LOST	AIRCRAFT LOST
August 1943	18	3	2
September 1943	95	14	4
October 1943	54	8	3
November 1943	5	-	-
December 1943	-	-	-
January 1944	-	-	-
February 1944	13	16	4
March 1944	13	-	2
April 1944	10	6	1
May 1944	24	-	-
June 1944	85	8	1
July 1944	106	-	1
August 1944	154	-	1
September 1944	155	28	12
October 1944	15	-	-
November 1944	24	6	1
December 1944	9	-	-

January 1945	-	-	-
February 1945	60	6	4
March 1945	44	12	3
April 1945	114	11	3
May 1945	142	6	1
Totals	1,140	124	43

Chop rate 3.7%

DATE	SORTIES	AIRCREW LOST	AIRCRAFT LOST
June 1945	70	1	-
July 1945	36	-	-
August 1945	59	-	-
September 1945	12	-	1
October 1945	30	-	-
November 1945	12	-	-
December 1945	-	-	-
January 1946	73	-	-
February 1946		NOT KNOWN	
March 1946	86	1	-
Totals	378	2	1

Appendix III: 196 Squadron Roll of Honour 1942-1946

THEIR NAMES LIVETH FOR EVERMORE

A plaque erected at Keevil airfield in commemoration off the crews who flew from there.

Sgt John Albert Austin	14 January 1943
Sgt William Robert Fisher	21 January 1943
F/Ltn Roderick Fairweather Milne	14 February 1943
P/O David Morgan Cross	14 February 1943
F/O Thomas Clinton Stuart Wood	14 February 1943
W/O Greaves Glen Clark	14 February 1943
F/Sgt John Duncan McIntyre	14 February 1943
F/O Neville Smart	26 February 1943
F/O Thomas Donald Gordon	26 February 1943
F/O Robert Lowell Benson	26 February 1943
Sgt George Alexander Aitken Ranken	26 February 1943

Sgt Dennis Herbert	26	February	1943
Sgt Henry Cavell Duckmanton	23	March	1943
Sgt Douglas Robert Jeffrey	23	March	1943
Sgt Basil John France Crook	23	March	1943
Sgt Samuel Robert Outra Hermon	23	March	1943
F/O Edward Richard Culff	29	March	1943
Sgt Thomas Albert Dew	29	March	1943
F/O Leslie Duncan McAllister	29	March	1943
Sgt Albert Charles August Veeck	29	March	1943
Sgt Hubert Roy Wilmore	29	Marc	1943
Sgt Arthur Lucas	29	March	1943
F/O Kenneth Flaxman Smart	29	March	1943
Sgt Arthur William Garnet Wilson	29	March	1943
F/Sgt Hugh Garfield Allen	29	March	1943
Sgt Denys Andrew	29	March	1943
Sgt Russell Verran Rosser DFM	14	April	1943
Sgt John Reginald Gallimore Calvert	14	April	1943
Sgt Dennis Charles Grocock	14	April	1943
Sgt Phillip Joseph Conwell	14	April	1943
Sgt Herbert Wilcock	14	April	1943
P/O Ivor Malcolm Payne Morgan	16	April	1943
F/Sgt Roy Hill	16	April	1943
P/O Albert William Arnold Trevarthen	16	April	1943

Sgt Norman Bruce	16	April	1943
Sgt Leslie Pickford	16	April	1943
Sgt George Frederick Fletcher	26	April	1943
Sgt Earnest George Francis	26	April	1943
Sgt Eric Thomas Dunn Hardee	26	April	1943
Sgt James Alfred Hawkins	26	April	1943
Sgt Frank Theodore Pratt	26	April	1943
Sgt Frederick Charles Swain	28	April	1943
Sgt Albert Wheatley	28	April	1943
Sgt Edward George Quick	28	April	1943
Sgt George Richard Burgess	28	April	1943
Sgt Edwin Donald Curling	28	April	1943
Sgt John Frederick Atkins	28	April	1943
Sgt Frank Guy	28	April	1943
Sgt Reginald Harry Taylor	28	April	1943
Sgt William McDonough	28	April	1943
Sgt Patrick William John Morrow	28	April	1943
F/Ltn Ian Numa Bonnard	28	April	1943
F/O John Joseph Wilfred Burns	28	April	1943
P/O Albert Robert Potter	28	April	1943
P/O Basil Arthur Curtis	28	April	1943
P/O John Ireland Pearson Ford	28	April	1943
Sgt John Staniforth	4	May	1943

Sgt Harry George Graham	4	May	1943
Sgt Ronald William Lynn	4	May	1943
Sgt George William Challoner James	4	May	1943
Sgt Bertie Edward Taylor	4	May	1943
F/Sgt Jack Greenfield	12	May	1943
F/Sgt Robert Burridge	12	May	1943
Sgt William O'Neill	12	May	1943
Sgt Kenneth Foster Bell	12	May	1943
Sgt William Eddington	12	May	1943
F/O Frank Whitford Jackson	12	June	1943
F/O Ronald Percy Lea	12	June	1943
P/O Noel Bentley Smythe	25	June	1943
P/O George William Pollard	25	June	1943
Sgt George Herbert William Peach	25	June	1943
Sgt Ronald Alfred Barlow	25	June	1943
F/O Eric Douglas Eastwood	3	July	1943
F/O Herbert Clifford Wheal	3	July	1943
F/Sgt Howard Langlands	3	July	1943
Sgt Alfred Reginald Stone	3	July	1943
Sgt Morris Dixon	3	July	1943
F/O James Henry Stewart	3	July	1943
F/Sgt Paul Gee	3	July	1943
Sgt Ronald Sydney Naile	3	July	1943

Sgt Allan Henry Taylor	3	July	1943
Sgt George Neville Downing	3	July	1943
Sgt Albert James Horne	3	July	1943
F/O Derrick Lionel Paul Justice	31	August	1943
Sgt Idris Llewellyn	31	August	1943
F/Sgt Charles Phillips Pierce	31	August	1943
P/O Frederick Norris	5	September	1943
P/O Richard Robert Whittaker	5	September	1943
F/Sgt Thomas Charles Foster	5	September	1943
Sgt Glynville William Moss	5	September	1943
F/O Kenneth Arthur Charles Ayling	5	September	1943
Sgt Francis Joseph Brown	5	September	1943
Sgt Avon Emrys Gomer Price	5	September	1943
F/Sgt Noel Nathaniel Wakely	16	September	1943
F/O Harold Allen Nelson Kitchen	16	September	1943
Sgt Alexander Sargant Taylor	16	September	1943
Sgt Stephen Thomas Flatman	16	September	1943
Sgt Wilfred Albert Gilbert	16	September	1943
Sgt Graham Francis Pyott	16	September	1943
Sgt Gordon Esmond Kane	16	September	1943
Sgt Thomas Lynas Dickie	3	October	1943
F/O James Lyall Deans DFC	17	October	1943
F/O Frederick John Chapman	17	October	1943

Sgt Kenneth Leonard Wallace	17	October	1943
Sgt James Lionel Lane	17	October	1943
Sgt Terence McDonnell	17	October	1943
F/Sgt Nolan Butts DFM	17	October	1943
F/Ltn John Gordon Griffiths	17	October	1943
W/O James Donaldson	4	February	1944
Sgt Robert Dowzer	4	February	1944
Sgt Kenneth Albert Glew	4	February	1944
Sgt Alfred Spray	4	February	1944
Sgt Kenneth Thomas Staple	4	February	1944
P/O Dennis Tunnard Vince	4	February	1944
P/O Henry Ivan Pryke	4	February	1944
F/O John Rothwell Lindley	5	February	1944
F/O Thomas Moore	5	February	1944
W/O Lionel Howard Woodruff	5	February	1944
W/O Calvert Hamilton Hunter	20	February	1944
W/O Charles Arthur Simpson	20	February	1944
Sgt John Edward Sawford	20	February	1944
F/Sgt Patrick William Sullivan	20	February	1944
F/Sgt Ronald Cecil Lysons	20	February	1944
Sgt Duncan Malcolm McCannell	20	February	1944
W/O John Hugh Lees	4	April	1944
Sgt Sidney Claypole	4	April	1944

Sgt Shayrene Meera	4	April	1944
F/Sgt Kenrick Payne	4	April	1944
F/O John Robert Teece	4	April	1944
F/Sgt John Thomas Wilkinson	4	April	1944
F/Ltn Fred Gribble	6	June	1944
F/O Alexander Edward Bothwell	6	June	1944
F/Sgt Phillip Charles Goddard	6	June	1944
Sgt Edward Whitehead	6	June	1944
Sgt Harry Edgar Wooton	6	June	1944
F/O Sydney Frank Yardley	6	June	1944
F/Ltn Richard Norman Parnell Luff DFM	6	June	1944
F/O James Kennedy Anderson	6	June	1944
F/O Dick Smith	30	June	1944
F/O Frank Douglas Chalkley	19	September	1944
Sgt Dennis Alec Matthews	19	September	1944
F/O George Henry Powderhill	19	September	1944
W/O Earnest Walter Bancroft	19	September	1944
F/Sgt Donovan Geoffrey Benning	19	September	1944
Sgt David Nicholson Clough	19	September	1944
F/Sgt Trevor Bowers Cragg	19	September	1944
F/Sgt Cyril Mabbott	20	September	1944
F/Sgt Andrew Joseph Murphy	20	September	1944
W/O William Robert Tait	20	September	1944

W/O Mark Azouz DFC	21	September	1944
F/Sgt David John Allaway	21	September	1944
F/Sgt Peter Harold Bode	21	September	1944
F/Sgt Robert Cowan	21	September	1944
F/Sgt Robert Walter Forrest	21	September	1944
F/O Reginald Cuthbert Gibbs	21	September	1944
F/Sgt Donald Hay Grant	21	September	1944
F/Sgt Charles Richard John Green	21	September	1944
F/Sgt Leonard Marsh	21	September	1944
F/Sgt Francis Ormson	21	September	1944
F/Sgt Richard Glyn Phillips	21	September	1944
F/Sgt John Sidney Poole	21	September	1944
Sgt Leslie Victor Ratcliffe	21	September	1944
F/Sgt Stanley Arthur Leonard Townsend	21	September	1944
F/Sgt Ronald Eric George Waltrich	21	September	1944
Sgt Gerald Desmond Patrick Kerton	24	September	1944
Sgt James Campbell Turreff	24	September	1944
Sgt Cedric Alfred Williamson	24	September	1944
F/O Derek William Eves	9	November	1944
Sgt Maurice Arthur Goult	9	November	1944
F/Sgt Charles Alfred Myers	9	November	1944
F/O John Anthony Norton	9	November	1944
F/Sgt Harry Ruston	9	November	1944

Name	Day	Month	Year
Sgt John Vaas Thompson	9	November	1944
W/C Maurice William L'isle La Valett Baker	21	February	1945
F/Sgt John Robert Gordon	21	February	1945
W/O John Bruce McGovern	21	February	1945
F/O Russell George Tickner	25	February	1945
F/Sgt George Alfred Humphrey	25	February	1945
W/O Joseph Daglish Stevenson	25	February	1945
W/O George Gregory Allman	31	March	1945
F/Sgt Frederick Charles Brenner	31	March	1945
F/Sgt Thomas Louttit Brunton	31	March	1945
P/O Clarence Campbell	31	March	1945
F/Sgt Derek Vivian Catterall	31	March	1945
F/Sgt John Richard Cross	31	March	1945
F/Sgt Paul Reginald Sergius Harding-Klimanek	31	March	1945
Sgt Kenneth William Linney	31	March	1945
F/Sgt Edward Sidney Lloyd	31	March	1945
F/Sgt Francis William Matthews	31	March	1945
Sgt Paul Montefiore Myers	31	March	1945
F/Sgt George Sidney Reed	31	March	1945
F/O Neville Carroll	3	April	1945
W/O Jack Grain	3	April	1945
F/Sgt Reginald Earnest Marshall	3	April	1945
W/O Gilbert Hughes	3	April	1945

W/O Stanley James Verse Philo	3	April	1945
W/O Kenneth Atkinson	11	April	1945
Sgt Robert Barnes	11	April	1945
Sgt Trevor Robert Jones	11	April	1945
Sgt Phillip Roy Tomlinson	11	April	1945
F/Sgt Frederick Vernon	11	April	1945
F/O James William Whitehead	11	April	1945
F/Sgt Harold Alfred Bell	10	May	1945
F/O John Leonard Breed	10	May	1945
F/Sgt Lionel James Douglas Gilyead	10	May	1945
W/O Raymond Charles Impett	10	May	1945
W/O Hugh Joseph Kilday	10	May	1945
F/Sgt David Welch	10	May	1945
Sgt Arthur Bennett	2	June	1945

Bibliography

1a. Primary Source

Public Records Office, Kew, Surrey.

AIR 27/1166: No. 196 Squadron ORB (10/42-6/44).

AIR 27 /1167: No. 196 Squadron ORB (7/44-3/46).

1b. Private Sources.

Correspondence with former aircrew and researchers listed in the acknowledgements section of this book

2. Secondary Sources

Books.

Bowyer, Michael J.F.   The Stirling bomber (Faber, 1980)

Falconer, Jonathan. Stirling Wings: The Short Stirling Goes To War (Stroud, Sutton Publishing 1995)

Falconer, Jonathan. Stirling at War (Ian Allan Ltd 1991)

Gomersall, Bryce. The Stirling File (Air-Britain Ltd 1979)

Holmes, Steve   Sherlock's Squadron (John Blake 2013)

Willis, Steve and Holliss, Barry. Military Airfields in the British Isles 1939-1945

(Omnibus Edition)

Websites

www.awm.gov.au   The Australian War Memorial

www.rafcommands.com   Royal Air Force Commands RAF Aircraft Serial Numbers Database

www.raf38group.org